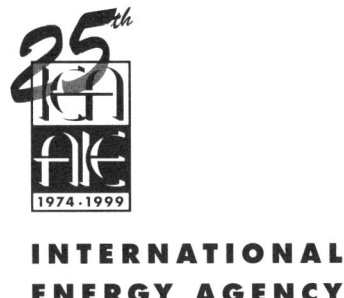

INTERNATIONAL ENERGY AGENCY

ENERGY MARKET REFORM

ELECTRICITY MARKET REFORM

An IEA Handbook

OECD
OCDE

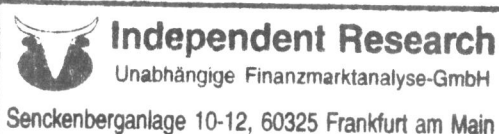

INTERNATIONAL ENERGY AGENCY
9, rue de la Fédération,
75739 Paris Cedex 15, France

The International Energy Agency (IEA) is an autonomous body which was established in November 1974 within the framework of the Organisation for Economic Co-operation and Development (OECD) to implement an international energy programme.

It carries out a comprehensive programme of energy co-operation among twenty four* of the OECD's twenty nine Member countries.
The basic aims of the IEA are:

■ To maintain and improve systems for coping with oil supply disruptions;

■ To promote rational energy policies in a global context through co-operative relations with non-Member countries, industry and international organisations;

■ To operate a permanent information system on the international oil market;

■ To improve the world's energy supply and demand structure by developing alternative energy sources and increasing the efficiency of energy use;

■ To assist in the integration of environmental and energy policies.

*IEA Member countries: Australia, Austria, Belgium, Canada, Denmark, Finland, France, Germany, Greece, Hungary, Ireland, Italy, Japan, Luxembourg, the Netherlands, New Zealand, Norway, Portugal, Spain, Sweden, Switzerland, Turkey, the United Kingdom, the United States. The European Commission also takes part in the work of the IEA.

ORGANISATION FOR ECONOMIC CO-OPERATION AND DEVELOPMENT

Pursuant to Article 1 of the Convention signed in Paris on 14th December 1960, and which came into force on 30th September 1961, the Organisation for Economic Co-operation and Development (OECD) shall promote policies designed:

■ To achieve the highest sustainable economic growth and employment and a rising standard of living in Member countries, while maintaining financial stability, and thus to contribute to the development of the world economy;

■ To contribute to sound economic expansion in Member as well as non-Member countries in the process of economic development; and

■ To contribute to the expansion of world trade on a multilateral, non-discriminatory basis in accordance with international obligations.

The original Member countries of the OECD are Austria, Belgium, Canada, Denmark, France, Germany, Greece, Iceland, Ireland, Italy, Luxembourg, the Netherlands, Norway, Portugal, Spain, Sweden, Switzerland, Turkey, the United Kingdom and the United States. The following countries became Members subsequently through accession at the dates indicated hereafter: Japan (28th April 1964), Finland (28th January 1969), Australia (7th June 1971), New Zealand (29th May 1973), Mexico (18th May 1994), the Czech Republic (21st December 1995), Hungary (7th May 1996), Poland (22nd November 1996) and the Republic of Korea (12th December 1996). The Commission of the European Communities takes part in the work of the OECD (Article 13 of the OECD Convention).

© OECD/IEA, 1999
Applications for permission to reproduce or translate all or part of this publication should be made to: Head of Publications Service, OECD
2, rue André-Pascal, 75775 Paris Cedex 16, France.

FOREWORD

The electricity supply industry is under reform in nearly all IEA countries. The new framework is characterised by the introduction of competition in electricity generation and end-user supply, new access to electricity networks and a redefinition of the regulatory function of governments.

This study describes the changes that are taking place in the industry and its regulatory structure, surveys the experience acquired so far, and identifies some key issues and lessons for the market-oriented reform of electricity supply.

Available evidence on liberalisation confirms the expectation of an improved economic performance of the sector, including lower costs and prices and increased consumer choice. However, along with economic efficiency, governments have to meet other public objectives, including security of supply and environmental protection. This study provides insights into how governments can successfully address this complex array of objectives in the new regulatory environment.

"Electricity Market Reform" is an update of a study conducted jointly by the OECD and the IEA as part of an overall project on regulatory reform. It was previously published as a chapter of "The OECD Report on Regulatory Reform" (OECD, 1997). The primary authors are Caroline Varley and Gudrun Lammers of the IEA. I thank IEA member countries for their helpful co-operation in providing and verifying factual information.

Robert Priddle
Executive Director

TABLE OF CONTENTS

1 INTRODUCTION — 9

2 OVERVIEW OF THE SECTOR — 11

General Economic Characteristics — 11
- Generation — 12
- Transmission — 13
- Distribution — 14
- Supply — 14
- Related Financial Markets — 15

Economic Importance and Security of Supply — 16

Electricity and the Environment — 18

A Brief History — 19
- 1870s - 1920s — 20
- 1920s - World War II — 20
- 1945 - 1960s — 20
- 1970s — 21
- 1980s - 1990s — 23

Current Situation — 25
- Industry Structure — 26
- Ownership — 28
- Current Regulatory Position and Indicators of Reform — 30

3 REGULATORY REFORM: KEY ISSUES — 37

Policy Objectives — 37

Industry Structure — 39

Ownership — 42

Models of Competition	**46**
▪ The Grid Access Model	46
▪ The Competitive Pool Model	47
▪ The Single Buyer Variation	48
▪ Evaluation of the Models	49
Related Financial Markets	**53**
Regulatory Structure	**57**
Pricing: the Transmission Grid	**58**
Pricing: End Users	**62**
Subsidies and Cross Subsidies	**65**
General Competition Law, Competitive Neutrality, State Aids	**67**
Security of Supply	**72**
▪ Short-Term Security of Transformation	72
▪ Long-Term Security of Transformation	74
▪ Security of Input Fuels	75
Environment	**77**
▪ Taxes and Fees	79
▪ Energy Subsidies	79
▪ Tradable Emissions Permits	81
▪ Energy Efficiency	83
Other Policy Objectives	**84**

4 REGULATORY REFORM: TRANSITION ISSUES — 87

Stranded Costs	**87**
Social Costs	**89**
Sequencing of Reforms	**90**
Evolution of Regulatory Reform	**90**

5 REGULATORY REFORM: WHAT DOES IT DELIVER? 93

Industry Performance 93

Consumer Benefits 95

6 CONCLUSIONS AND RECOMMENDATIONS 97

Conclusions 97

Recommendations 98

BIBLIOGRAPHY 103

LIST OF TABLES

1.	Electricity Sector Structure in OECD Countries	27
2.	Ownership Patterns in OECD Countries	29
3.	Indicators of Which End-users are Legally Permitted to Choose Supplier	31
4.	Indicators of Regulatory Status	32-33
5.	Ownership of Regional Electricity Companies in England and Wales	70

LIST OF BOXES

1.	Structure of the Power Sector Supply Chain	16
2.	Example of Electricity Price Influencing Location	17
3.	A Brief History	25
4.	Contracts for Differences: An Illustration of Spot Market Price Risk Reduction	56

INTRODUCTION

This study forms part of an overall project on regulatory reform initiated by the OECD, as well as part of the ongoing work programme of the IEA. A main purpose of the OECD project is to disseminate some of the "lessons learned" in earlier reform experiences.

Electric power is essential to modern life. It fuels much of industry, the incubator of the new-born, the computers of the commodity trader and the railways of the commuter. It is an input to almost all goods and services. At the same time, power generation and its end use have negative environmental effects and may be implicated in global warming.

Since the middle of the century this central importance of electricity has been recognised by governments. Until very recently, most governments have also considered the whole power sector to be a natural monopoly and therefore that it should be closely regulated.

Regulatory reform of this sector offers significant potential benefits in terms of improved efficiency in the production of electricity and in the allocation of resources across the economy, lower prices for consumers, improved risk allocation, and stimulus to economic growth and competitiveness. If it is done well, these potential benefits are enormous. As with some other basic infrastructure and capital-intensive industries, investments made in the sector and by electricity users are long-lived; decisions made today have far-reaching and long-lived effects.

The central focus of recent regulatory reform has been the introduction of competition into the generation and supply sub-sectors of the electricity sector through market liberalisation. Market liberalisation critically shifts decision making from the state — or state-influenced entities — to the market and, often for the first time, gives consumers a choice. The evidence to date supports the strong expectation of a much better economic performance of the sector; it also shows that reform can result in lower costs and a broader array of choices to consumers. However, there are other public policy objectives underlying liberalisation. It is important that these objectives, such as security of supply, environmental performance and social equity are met — hopefully bettered — in the new conditions. Evidence to date shows that these objectives can be met under the new competitive market conditions, but it is critical that they be included in liberalisation efforts at the beginning of the process.

Gas regulation is not addressed here. Gas and electricity are substitutes for many end-users and gas is an input into the generation of electric power. Hence, the regulatory status of one sector influences the other sector. A more complete analysis was not possible within the constraints of this study.

This study provides, first, an overview of the power sector (Section 2). The main part of the report (Section 3) considers the key issues in regulatory reform. It highlights the importance of identifying the underlying objectives of reform, before reviewing the mechanisms for introducing reform and competition. This section also considers the key public policy objectives of security of supply and protection of the environment and how these objectives can be met in the new conditions. Section 4 considers transition issues

In Section 5 a preliminary attempt is made to answer the question: What does regulatory reform and market liberalisation actually deliver? The report ends with conclusions and recommendations to governments.

OVERVIEW OF THE SECTOR

General Economic Characteristics

Electricity has a number of features which distinguish it from other energy products — and from most other commodities. First, electricity demand fluctuates in a daily and seasonal pattern, with superimposed random variations, largely (but not entirely) due to the fact that much of it is consumed in weather-related uses (heating and cooling). Second, it is not storable in large amounts and at low cost, which means that power at one point in time is not a good substitute for power at another point in time. Hence, power production and supply are multiple time-differentiated products. Third, the cost of load exceeding supply, brownouts or blackouts, is considerable. Taken together, these features create what is known as a "peak load (demand) problem": if all load must be supplied, then capacity must equal or exceed load at all times. Otherwise, random supply interruptions can occur in the form of brownouts or blackouts, causing considerable economic damage.

Another important feature of electricity demand is that it requires further transformation into the desired final form of energy: light, heat, cooling or motion power. This is due to the versatility of electric power. Hence, some of the input energies to electricity, e.g. natural gas, are also its competitors in end energy markets. Also, in many cases, demand is not very price elastic in the short term because a customer's transformation equipment (e.g. household goods like freezers) is relatively long-lived.

Electricity supply assets (including generating capacity) are also long-lived. The typical lifetime of nuclear plants is now expected to be 40 years, and hydro-electric plants, including dams, are expected to remain in service much longer.[1] Installed assets are accretions

---

[1]. Another example is Joskow (1983), for example, who illustrates the point by reference to a set of 588 large fossil-fuelled steam electric generating plants operating in 1979 in the United States. Of those for which the initial date of operation was given, 40 per cent began operation before 1950 and 17 per cent before 1940. He notes that most very old plants have been substantially modified in the intervening years.

over a long period of time during which technology, relative prices, beliefs about future demand and prices, economic and environmental regulation, population and industry have changed. Hence, actual installations are not those judged "optimal" under present conditions.

It is helpful to divide the supply side into four parts: generation, transmission, distribution and supply. Traditionally, the sector was considered as consisting of the first three parts: generation, transmission and distribution. These parts show clear differences in their functions, technology, and cost characteristics. More recently, however, power sector reform has encouraged the emergence of supply, or retailing, of electricity to ultimate consumers, as a separate and distinct function.[2]

■ Generation

Generation is the transformation of some other form of energy into electric energy, either chemically through the combustion of fossil fuel such as coal, oil or gas, or physically through the use of nuclear fission, or kinetic energy from wind or water in motion.[3] Different types of generating plants are characterised by different shares of fixed and variable cost: hydro-electric, nuclear and some renewable plants have high fixed cost (essentially capacity) and low variable cost (essentially fuel). Fuel cost in nuclear generation varies between 4 per cent (Canada) to 23 per cent (Japan) in OECD Member Countries.[4] In contrast, fuel accounts for 22 per cent (certain regions of North America) to 53 per cent (Germany) of total generating cost. The fuel share of gas-based generating cost lies between 46 per cent (Canada) and 75 per cent (parts of the United States).

---

2. *There are a number of additional functions, such as system operation/dispatch/network control and spot and contractual markets. However, the distinction according to the above mentioned four categories is the one that is most evident, due to the different functional and cost characteristics of those steps.*

3. *Many renewable energy sources actually use other processes. Fuel cells, for example, use fossil fuels, but the energy is extracted physically.*

4. *At a 10 per cent discount rate, 30 years lifetime and 75 per cent load factor. OECD Nuclear Energy Agency (NEA) / International Energy Agency (IEA): Projected Cost of Generating Electricity. 1992 Update. Paris, 1993.*

This cost structure means that there is an order for plant dispatch, the so-called "merit order", which minimises total costs, bringing plant into operation as demand rises (*i.e.* no more than is necessary to meet demand at any given time). Hence, in a cost-based system, capacity with low variable and high fixed cost, such as nuclear, is operated as much as possible. This type of capacity is called base load. The reverse holds for the type of gas plants referred to above, which are operated at peak or intermediate load. Since load varies rapidly and unpredictably, so does system cost.

■ Transmission

Transmission is the high-voltage transport of electricity. Most modern transmission systems in industrialised nations are more or less densely meshed, allow power exchanges over large distances and, thereby, establish an electricity system featuring power trade, least-cost operation of geographically dispersed plants, bundling of demand and pooling of reserve capacity. These features mean that in most locations, electricity traded over the grid is vastly cheaper than locally generated power.[5]

A modern, synchronously interconnected transmission system also requires minute-to-minute co-ordination among generators and grid owners in order to protect it from damage. Voltage and frequency fluctuations have to be maintained within a very narrow band. In the wires, electricity flows along the lines of least electrical resistance, not along contractual paths, and towards "load valleys". This means that the technical problems one generator experiences, or the transactions he carries out with a consumer, may affect third parties not involved in the transaction. That is, there are significant externalities which make the transmission grid a natural monopoly over a relatively large geographic area. For these reasons, and in order to avoid breakdown in all or part of

---

5. *There are, however, some thinly populated areas in OECD Member countries where grid electricity is more expensive than decentralised generation. These are seen to be important niche markets for renewable energies.*

the system, generators are required to deliver so-called ancillary services, which can consist of voltage or frequency support, "spinning reserve",[6] or "black start" capability to re-start the system after a breakdown. This requirement for close co-ordination among operators of the transmission grid and generators gives rise to economies of vertical integration between these two parts of the industry. Such co-ordination is a key constraint on possible structural change in the sector. However, reformers — in, for example, the United Kingdom and the state of Victoria, Australia, as well as independent power producers elsewhere — have found mechanisms for the co-ordination of generation and transmission under separate ownership or management. This separation has been shown to be feasible. The issue remains whether total costs are lower under vertical separation (this is explored later).

■ Distribution

Distribution is the low-voltage transport of electricity, generally from the transmission system to the end-user, or between generators and end users. Distribution often shows strong economies of density in urban agglomerations but diseconomies in remote areas. Distribution is a natural monopoly over given geographic areas.

■ Supply

Supply is the contracting for, and selling of, electricity to end-users. Supply also includes metering and billing, and can comprise activities such as customer information, advice and financing. Supply is not a natural monopoly. It can be wholesale or retail. This report does not clearly distinguish these categories since they are subject to further research at the OECD and IEA.

To give an idea of relative cost magnitudes, generation in the United Kingdom accounts for about 65 per cent of total cost of

---

6. *Power plants where the (gas or steam) turbine is rotating but not the generating unit. They thus consume fuel as if they were producing but are not. However, run in this mode, they can be brought into operation very quickly.*

the supply chain; transmission, 10 per cent; distribution, 20 per cent; and supply, 5 per cent (Newbery and Green, 1996, p. 59).

■ Related Financial Markets

Where markets for electric power have been established, new financial markets have also become established. Electricity contracts range from long-term (e.g., 20 years) requirements contracts to short-term (e.g., one-half hour) supply contracts. Built upon these underlying assets are futures contracts and options. In dynamic commodity markets, like those for grains and petroleum, financial markets enable the risk of price volatility to be shifted away from the parties least able to manage them (the end-user) to intermediaries. Electricity, as has already been demonstrated in the American gas market, is conducive to such intermediation. In certain liberalised electricity markets, this risk intermediation already includes the availability of futures contracts, options and their derivatives.

The different parts of the electricity supply industry are vertically or complementarily related but their relationships are, in fact, more complex. For example, transmission and generation are complements, since in most cases, transmission is necessary to connect generators to end users. However, increasing transmission capacity can also be a substitute for additional generating capacity, since it may allow power to be obtained from a distant generator. As mentioned above, transmission allows merit order dispatch, but it also amalgamates demand and thus allows the use of larger plant and the exploitation of economies of scale. Demand patterns vary between regions. The larger the interconnected area, the more individual demand fluctuations offset each other, leading to greater use of (comparatively) low-cost base load capacity, and increased sharing of peak and reserve capacity. Transmission makes possible greater exploitation of economies of scale in generation and risk-sharing of load fluctuations. The larger the interconnected area, the cheaper (on average) the supply, until the cost reductions are outweighed by rising transmission cost, including grid losses.

These cost and demand relationships between generation and transmission, along with the economies of vertical integration between transmission and generation, give rise to a complex relationship between the two activities.

Another example of the complexity of relationships among the four main functions of the sector is that between generation and supply, where interruptible supply contracts can be a substitute for additional transmission or generating capacity.

Box 1

Structure of the Power Sector Supply Chain

Function	Fraction of total cost (in the United Kingdom)*
1. Generation: transformation of other energy into electric energy. Potentially competitive	**65 %**
2. Transmission: High voltage transport of electricity. Natural monopoly features (at present)	**10 %**
3. Distribution: Low voltage transport of electricity to end user. Natural monopoly features for given geographic area	**20 %**
4. Supply: Retailing of electricity to end users. Potentially competitive	**5 %**

*Source for cost estimates: Newbery and Green, 1996, p. 59.

Economic Importance and Security of Supply

The electricity sector in itself is an important part of a modern society's economy, leaving aside its importance as an input to other goods and services. In the United States, for example, annual sales of electric power total over $200 billion. The electric power industry accounts for about 3.2 per cent GDP and about 5 per cent of gross capital stock (1994). In France, Electricité de France, which effectively constitutes the industry, had annual sales (in 1995) of 188.6 billion francs and it employed 117,000. As noted earlier, electricity is, at the same time, a critical and, for many uses, a non-substitutable input to other goods and services. It is an input to all industrial production, as well as to key services such as telecommunications and transport systems. It powers many of the elements of modern life such as computers and freezers. It is a key purchaser of outputs from other industries, such as coal and terminal equipment.

For the overwhelming majority of industrial and service end users, however, electricity makes up less than 5 per cent of total cost. Only a small group of industries is very electricity intensive. These are first and foremost aluminium smelters, but also glassworks and some chemical plants. For such industries, relative electricity prices are a main factor in choice of location.

Box 2

Example of Electricity Price Influencing Location

A glassworks company, the Schott Group, has over the past decade reduced the number of its employees in Germany by 1,000 to 11,000 and added 3,000 jobs abroad. Glassworks are relatively energy intensive; hence, the company's cost of running its furnaces are 60 per cent lower in the United States and 30 per cent lower in France and the Czech Republic, where electricity charges are significantly lower than in Germany.

(Wall Street Journal, 12/13 July 1996, p. 1)

The economic importance, and the non-substitutable nature, of electricity in many uses, means that governments have for a long time been concerned to ensure that there is security of electricity supply — both in the short and the long term. It remains a fundamental objective of public policy in OECD countries to ensure that security of supply is sustained, although the means to achieve this objective is undergoing radical reappraisal in the context of regulatory reform and the introduction of market liberalisation.

There is also international trade and investment in the industry. Among IEA countries, the largest net exporters of electric power are France and Canada, exporting in 1993 about 60 TWh and 30 TWh, respectively. Since these are net figures, they mask significantly higher gross power flows across borders. However, less than 8 per cent of power supplied in European IEA countries was imported. The United States imports only about 1 per cent of its electric power, mostly from Canada (IEA, 1995).[7] Many Asian Pacific countries cannot import electricity from other countries because of their geographical locations. Utilities also export services or expertise, and invest directly abroad. For example, Electricité de France is building infrastructure projects totalling $11.6 billion in Argentina, Belgium, China, Ivory Coast, Gabon, Guinea-Bissau, Mali, Poland, Portugal and Spain (So and Shin, 1996, p. 11).

Electricity and the Environment

The power sector has a very significant effect on the environment, locally, regionally and globally. Environmental impacts of the power sector include emissions of carbon dioxide, sulphur dioxide and nitrogen oxides. In the OECD area electric power generation in 1990 led to the emission of 30 million tonnes of sulphur oxides, 10 million tonnes of nitrogen oxides and nearly four billion tones of carbon dioxide (OECD 1993). In the United Kingdom the power sector is the main producer of man-made carbon dioxide and of sulphur dioxide, and the second largest sectoral producer of nitrogen oxides (Armstrong, Cowan and Vickers pp. 280-1).

---

7. The implications of electricity market opening and competition in large regions were analysed in a IEA document entitled "Inter-system Competition and Trade in Electricity - Implications for the Environment and Environmental Policy" (IEA/SLT(95)25, unpublished). The analysis of the economics of electricity trade flows shows that while market opening may result in a short-term boost, electricity trade can be expected to fall back to relatively low levels again in the mid- to long run, since it is cheaper to transport input energies (including natural gas) and transform them into electricity close to the point of use than to transport electricity over long distances.

The power sector is therefore a large source of pollutants causing acid rain and greenhouse gas effects and has a major part to play in addressing the climate change problem. Governments are concerned to find cost effective policies that will minimise emissions. This has direct implications for the types of fuel used for power generation (some fuels have a much better emissions performance than others) and for the types of plants which are built. It should be noted that the objective of minimising greenhouse gas emissions may not be fully compatible with energy security concerns. For example, coal has been subsidised with the aim of increasing security of supply in some OECD countries, such as Germany, but it causes high sulphur oxides, carbon dioxide and other emissions.

Other environmental impacts of power generation include heat injected in rivers through water used as a coolant, the visual unsightliness of high voltage transmission lines, the mining and transport of primary (input) fuels and the risks associated with the operation of nuclear power plants and management of spent nuclear fuel.

Environmental regulation is generally considered necessary to address these issues, even in a context of liberalised markets, because environmental effects are often externalities, *i.e.*, are not borne by those who cause them. Regulatory reform both of the regulations governing the electricity sector and of environmental regulations need careful handling against this background. Governments will be concerned to ensure that environmental objectives can be met cost effectively whatever the framework conditions for the power sector.

A Brief History

The power sector has existed for over 100 years. Throughout this time, it has experienced waves of change in structure and regulatory approach driven by technical and economic developments. The key evolutionary stages are outlined below.

■ 1870s - 1920s

At the outset, the developing industry was much more fragmented than it is now. It was largely privately owned, and, at least in many parts of Europe, not subject to effective regulation. Development of the grid was still very limited and areas of dense load, such as major cities or industrial sites were in some cases subject to fierce competition among suppliers who had to provide the infrastructure as well as supply. Industrial auto-production was much more common in the first half of the century.

■ 1920s - World War II

The first attempts by national or local governments to guide the market came in the 1920s and 1930s. Governments were beginning to view electric power less as a luxury and more as an everyday necessity. This period saw the construction of large, publicly-financed and publicly-owned hydro-electric projects. Electrification programmes extended the geographic coverage of the grid, especially to rural areas. The industry included a large number of companies, private and public, small and large, many owning and operating distribution facilities. Transmission remained fragmented, in many cases lacking interconnection and with inadequate overall network control, resulting in large grid losses and uncertain supply.

■ 1945 - 1960s

This was a period of dramatic change in which already developed economic concepts began to be applied universally to deal with the negative economic behaviour which then characterised much of the industry — price wars, cartels, and other anticompetitive oligopolistic behaviour. At the same time, technical progress was changing the economics of power generation and transmission. The minimum efficient plant size increased dramatically, at the same time as transmission and distribution grids were nearing completion. The increasing economies of scale rendered many of the old, small power companies uneconomic.

Many European governments concluded that the entire sector was a natural monopoly (which had already been suggested by Thomas Edison himself), the multitude of small producers had to be merged in a single nation-wide monopoly, or several large regional, monopolies. They felt that the best way to prevent monopolistic behaviour was to place these in public ownership. France decided to create EdF in 1946. Italy was the last European country to follow this trend by creating the state-owned monopoly ENEL in 1962. Since the industry was believed to be a natural monopoly, many countries enacted legislation that either explicitly forbade new entry into the power sector or exempted it from general competition law. Australia and New Zealand adopted a similar model. One of the notable exceptions to this rule in Europe is Spain, where statutory entry barriers were never erected, and where there continued to be some competition, especially in the region around Barcelona.

In the United States, a different model prevailed — the private monopoly regulated by an independent regulatory commission. Nevertheless, from the era of public hydro construction and electrification programmes, a large number of federal or municipally-owned power companies remained — and remain — in business in the United States.

■ 1970s

It was in the United States that the first doubts emerged as to whether the chosen model of the regulated monopoly utility worked efficiently. As early as 1962, Averch and Johnson showed that a private monopoly subject to rate-of-return regulation had incentives to overinvest in capital assets.[8] Subsequently, a whole literature developed around the issues of regulatory "capture" (regulators might seek employment later on with the companies they regulate, and thus fail to regulate them properly), optimal regulatory lags, etc.

The 1970s was the decade of the oil shocks, which raised the price of what was at that time the key input fuel to electric power. This

---

8. Averch, H. and Johnson, L.L.: Behaviour of the Firm under Regulatory Constraint. In: American Economic Review, Vol. 52, 1962.

prompted a number of countries to step up the pace of existing nuclear programmes, in some cases dramatically, and others to embark on such programmes for the first time. There were simultaneous efforts to substitute coal for oil, and near prohibition of the use of gas and oil-fired power generation in the United States, Europe and Japan.

During this energy crisis, a critical discovery was made — independent generators can operate in a manner that does not destroy the stability of the grid. Along with changes in the minimum efficient scale in generation, described above and below, this implied that other structures than a vertically integrated monopoly were possible.

During this period, other changes were occurring in the sector. First, the real cost of nuclear generation rose substantially due to inflationary expectations. At the same time, citizens in many countries expressed increased concern about the safety of nuclear plant operation and disposal of spent fuel. This resulted in the adoption of additional safety measures, the expectation of increased future costs associated with existing plants, and an increased perception of the risk of such operations. Second, the price of natural gas in the United States fell substantially with the regulatory reform of that sector. This further diminished minimum efficient scale for generation. Third, the petroleum cost increases caused much greater cost consciousness and prompted further research into power generating cost. This research showed that, depending on the country, the era of large efficient scales for fossil generation was over. During the 1950s and 1960s, a combination of improved thermal efficiencies and technical progress had shifted the minimum efficient scale of new generating units towards ever larger sizes. However, between the mid-1970s and the mid-1980s, this trend ended (For nuclear plants, unit minimum efficient scale remained over 1,000 MW and at multi-unit plant-level the minimum efficient scale was even larger).[9]

---

9. Krautmann, A. C., and Solow, J. C.: *Economies of Scale in Nuclear Power Generation.* In: *Southern Economic Journal,* Vol. 55, No. 1, 1988.

Other research suggested that the generation side of the power business was perhaps not a natural monopoly anymore, and raised the question whether it ever had been. Some studies at *company* level showed the minimum efficient size to be amazingly small.[10] This result only holds if companies trade with each other efficiently, especially if there is a mechanism that ensures optimal, cost-minimising dispatch of all power plants in the market, and if the *market is big enough* to reap the benefits of bundling demand.

Yet other research found relatively large economies of vertical integration between generation and the grid, especially transmission.[11] These are due to the complex technical and economic interdependence between generation and transmission. These economies of vertical integration meant that if the power industry were to be organised competitively, mechanisms had to be found to provide the overall co-ordination and co-operation needed to protect the system and ensure optimal interaction between transmission and generation.

■ 1980s - 1990s

Pressure built up to reform the power sector, driven by a number of factors which varied from country to country. A fundamental influence was the changing economics of the industry, due to changes in the costs of nuclear and coal-fired generation, and the development of the combined cycle gas turbine (CCGT). In addition to the changed costs of generation — which had the effect of diminishing minimum efficient scale for generation — steadily decreasing information technology (IT) costs have reduced the price of sophisticated metering and grid control equipment, thus facilitating decentralisation of supply.

---

10. *One often-quoted study is that by Christensen and Greene, who estimate the size of the optimal power company at only 4,000 MW. While there are indications that the study may underestimate optimal company size, other studies support the evidence that optimal firm size may be smaller than anticipated, and that very large power companies, some of which are 10 to 20 times as large as the quoted figure, may operate at diseconomies of scale. See Christensen, L. R., and Greene, W. H.: Economies of scale in United States Electric Power generation. In: Journal of Political Economy, No. 84, 1976.*

11. *See e.g. Henderson, J. S.: Cost Estimation for Vertically Integrated Firms: The Case of Electricity. In: Crew, M. A.: Analysing the Impact of Regulatory Change in Public Utilities. Lexington, Mass./Toronto, 1985.*

In addition to these technologically driven changes in costs, there was an increased influence of market-oriented economic thinking and a growing emphasis on the need to find ways to maximise economic efficiency against a background of growing pressure on state budgets and faltering macro-economic performance. In many countries electricity prices were perceived as excessively high, as compared with prices elsewhere. Another key driver in some countries was to generate revenues from privatisation of the industry, which was also expected to improve efficiency.

The CCGT resulted from a spillover of technology used in military jet aircraft engines. New materials and design enabled gas turbines to burn fuels at much higher temperatures, increasing efficiency, and also allowed the combination of simple gas turbines with a heat recovery steam generator (HRSG) and a steam turbine to yield the CCGT. This discovery has pushed the boundary of achievable thermal efficiency to 60 per cent and has shifted the minimum efficient plant size down from approximately 1,000 MW in the early 1980s to much lower values - between 50 and 350 MW according to some authors, to even smaller units according to others.[12]

There is presently a cost advantage for CCGTs over other power plants. In particular, whereas single cycle gas turbines tended to be operated in peak load, CCGTs have become the baseload generating option of choice in almost all member countries of the IEA.

In the early 1990s, the United Kingdom, Argentina and Norway embarked on far-reaching reforms of their power sectors. These reforms have helped to develop the practical mechanisms needed to underpin the changes, such as the trading mechanisms needed to balance competition on the one hand and co-operation on the other. There are, however, several models of competition and some of the issues around the various approaches are still subject to debate.

---

12. See e.g. Bayless, C.: *Less is More - Why Gas Turbines Will Transform Electric Utilities*. In: *Public Utilities Fortnightly*, December 1, 1994.

> **Box 3**
>
> ## A Brief History
>
> | | |
> |---|---|
> | *1870s - 1920s:* | Private ownership. Fragmentation. No universal grid. |
> | *1920s - World War II:* | Governments recognition of electric power as a "necessity". Public investment but industry remains fragmented. |
> | *World War II - 1960s:* | Sector viewed as a natural monopoly. Some governments consolidate and nationalise the power sector; others apply economic regulation; some exempt the sector from the application of competition law. |
> | *1970s:* | Oil shocks. Changes in fuel inputs to power generation and shift toward nuclear. Experience with independent power producers on the public grid and discovery that minimum efficient scale of generation may be smaller. Identification of economies of vertical integration between generation and transmission. |
> | *1980s - 1990s:* | CCGT development reduces minimum efficient scale in generation; coordination eased by falling information technology costs. Power sector reform in some countries involved the development of competition in generation and supply. |

Current Situation

Regulatory reform of the power sector involves a complex interplay of factors. There is a dynamic relationship between restructuring, ownership changes, regulatory changes, changes in regulatory institutions and the introduction of competition. Restructuring, and changes in ownership and in regulatory institutions are likely to be prerequisites for the introduction of competition, especially if the industry is highly concentrated horizontally and vertically-integrated. The nature of reform crucially depends on the starting point. This section therefore gives a brief description of where OECD countries are at this stage in the evolution of the power sector.

■ Industry Structure

Industry structure varies widely between OECD countries. Historically, some countries took deliberate action to restructure the sector and bring it closer to what was perceived as the optimal company size at the time, whereas others let the industry develop its own dynamics — within the framework of protected monopoly utilities. In some countries, horizontal and vertical integration improved system co-ordination and (co-operative) trade over past performance; in others, the structure of the power sector is fragmented and resembles its state of development during the first half of the century. In some cases very small firms have survived, operating far below the minimum efficient size, as well as markets so small that they are not of cost-minimising dispatch scale. Although the power sector's long history shows that restructuring may take place for other reasons than the introduction of competition, it is the latter which has been the driver of recent restructuring programmes in nearly all reforming OECD countries. In some countries this has taken the form of industry consolidation. This is the case for the Netherlands power sector, especially the distribution business in the late 1980s, because many distributors were operating far below the optimal firm size, and the market had failed to integrate nation-wide cost-minimising dispatch. This led to large price disparities across the country. Today, the Dutch government is considering further consolidation.

Table 1 (p. 27) gives an overview of current industry structure in OECD Member countries. It shows an enormous degree of diversity: a country like Switzerland with seven million inhabitants and roughly 15 GW installed capacity has 1,200 electricity supply companies, mostly small municipal or cantonal distributors, whereas neighbouring France with a population of 58 million people and approximately 108 GW capacity is supplied, exclusively, by the state-owned company EDF. All other countries lie between these extremes.

Table 1
Electricity Sector Structure in OECD Countries

	Degree of Horizontal Integration			Vertical Integration
	Generation	Transmission	Distribution	
Australia	mixed*↘	high	mixed*↘	mixed*↘
Austria	moderate	moderate	moderate	high
Belgium	high	high	moderate	low
Canada	moderate	moderate	moderate	high
Denmark	low	moderate	low	moderate**
Finland	moderate/high	moderate/high	moderate	moderate**
France	high	high	high	high
Germany	moderate	moderate	low	mixed
Greece	high	high	high	high
Ireland	high	high	high	high
Italy	high	high	high	high↘
Japan	moderate	moderate	moderate	high
Netherlands	moderate↗	high	low	moderate**
New Zealand	moderate↘	high	low	low
Norway	low	high	low	low
Portugal	high↘	high	moderate	low
Spain	moderate↘	high	moderate	moderate**
Sweden	moderate	high	moderate	low
Switzerland	low	moderate	low	low
Turkey	high	high	high	high
England & Wales	moderate↘	high	low	low
United States	low	low	low	mixed

* "Mixed" means that different utilities have starkly different degrees of integration.
** "Moderate" means that the four main activities (generation, transmission, distribution and supply) are not fully vertically integrated within each utility.
Source: IEA.

2 OVERVIEW OF THE SECTOR

■ Ownership

The starting point differs widely in OECD countries. In the United Kingdom, France, and Italy, the electricity supply industry was nationalised after World War II in a conscious effort to improve its performance since public ownership was seen as a means to make utilities work for "the public interest".[13] There was an expectation that they would not engage in behaviour characteristic of private monopolies with a profit motive, especially setting excessively high monopoly prices. Regulatory oversight was absent or, in some cases, extremely weak. In some countries, oversight was directly carried out by government institutions not sufficiently independent from general economic and social policy objectives. This produced results such as below-cost electricity prices as a means to control inflation during the high-inflation, high-unemployment period of the 1970s. State-owned utilities, especially when they were large, were also prone to over-staffing.

Table 2 (p. 29) gives an overview of current ownership patterns in OECD Member countries. The situation in Member countries is more complex, since "public ownership" can mean ownership at national, federal, provincial, cantonal or municipal level, or even ownership by consumer co-operatives as in some cases in the US or in Denmark. The situation also reveals major differences of approach in restructuring.

Large-scale privatisation was undertaken in Australia (Victoria) and the United Kingdom; in both cases, nearly the entire power sector has now been privatised. New Zealand did not consider privatising but instead corporatised its power sector. Norway corporatised transmission and the part of generation that is owned by the national State.

---

13. *In some cases, utilities' statutes contained an explicit obligation to further the public interest. This was the case for the United Kingdom's Central Electricity Generating Board (CEGB).*

Table 2
Ownership Patterns in OECD Countries

Predominantly Public	Mixed	Predominantly Private
Australia (New South Wales, Queensland, South Australia, Tasmania, Western Australia)		Australia (Victoria)
	Austria	
	Belgium (distribution)	Belgium (generation, transmission)
Canada		
	Denmark	
	Finland	
France		
	Germany	
Greece		
Ireland		
Italy		
		Japan
Netherlands		
New Zealand		
Norway		
Portugal		
		Spain
	Sweden	
Switzerland (distribution)	Switzerland (generation, transmission)	
Turkey		
		United Kingdom
	United States	

■ Current Regulatory Position and Indicators of Reform

Some countries that have reformed their electricity sector allow end-users to choose their electricity supplier. In many cases, this participation in the market is not extended to all end-users at once. Table 3 (p. 31) provides information, for selected countries, about which end-users are legally free to choose suppliers. Note that the European Union rules set a minimum pace for its Member States. It should also be noted that the legal ability to choose one's supplier does not necessarily mean that users find it economically beneficial to switch suppliers; there may be significant switching costs, such as the forced purchase of a sophisticated meter.

Table 4 (p. 32/33) provides further information, for selected countries, about ownership, obligations to transmit, the nature of the price control regime, the independence of the regulator (if there is one), and whether the sector is subject to general competition law. More specific information about some of these jurisdictions is provided in the country annex. It should be noted that a table such as this cannot present nuances that may constitute the difference between an effective legal regime and an ineffective one.

Table 3
Indicators of Which End-users are Legally Permitted to Choose Supplier

Above what level of use are users permitted to choose their own supplier of electricity?

Country or State	First step Year	First step Minimum	Second step Year	Second step Minimum	Third step Year	Third step Minimum	Fourth step Year	Fourth step Minimum
Australia								
New South Wales	10/1996	40 GWh/yr	4/1997	4 GWh/yr	7/1997	750 Mwh/yr	1999	0
Queensland	1998	40 GWh/yr	1999	4 GWh/yr	2000	200 Mwh/yr	2001	0
Victoria***	1994	5 MW	1995	1 MW	1996	750 MWh/yr	1998	160 MWh/yr
Canada								
Alberta	none							
European Union	1999	100 GWh*	2000	*	2003	*		
Finland*	1995	500 KW	1997	0				
France*	none							
Germany****	1998	0						
New Zealand 500 KW	1993	not over	1994	all				
Norway	1991	0						
Spain*****	1998	15 GWh	2000	9 GWh	2002	5 GWh	2004	1 GWh
Sweden	1996	0						
United Kingdom*	1990	1 MW	1994	100 kW	1998	0		
United States								
California	2002**	0**						
New Hampshire	1998	0						

* Pursuant to the Directive on Common Rules for the Internal Market in Electricity, each Member State has to open up its market progressively in accordance with a set formula. This requires that, by 1999 all customers who use more than 100 GWh per year will be free to choose independent or foreign EU suppliers. With respect to end users smaller than 100 GWh, see EU Directive on Electricity Liberalisation below.

** The law requires all users to have access by 1 January 2002, but this may occur sooner and may be preceded by a phase-in.

*** In Victoria, at the fifth step in January 2001, all users will be free to choose their supplier.

**** Municipalities can restrict choice until 2003 under certain conditions.

***** All users will have access after 2007.

Table 4
Indicators of Regulatory Status

1. What is the ownership/management relationship between the transmission grid and generation?
2. Is the owner of the transmission grid obligated to transmit power for third parties?
3. What is the price control regime for those prices which are controlled?
4. Is there an independent regulator?
5. Is the sector subject to the general competition law?

Country or State	Answer 1	Answer 2	Answer 3	Answer 4	Answer 5
Australia New South Wales	separate State-owned entities	yes	transmission and distribution to be more cost-reflective; mix of CPI-X revenue and price caps	yes	yes
Victoria	no	yes	transmission and distribution to be more cost-reflective; mix of CPI-X revenue and price caps	yes	yes
Canada Alberta	vertically integrated over local regions		legislated hedge easing into none		
British Columbia	same State-owned utility	yes	cost-of-service rate-of-return and performance-based/incentive	yes	
Czech Republic	67 % State-owned utility	n.a.	all prices set by Min. Finance		yes
Finland*	separate company; 2 biggest generators own 50 %, state and various others own rest	yes	no price regulation; prices monitored by a regulatory authority	yes, accountable to the Min. Trade and Industry	yes
France*	vertically integrated	no*			
Germany*	often vertically integrated over local regions	no*	Länder Ministries of Economic Affairs	no	no**

* Under the Directive on Common Rules for the Internal Market in Electricity, the owner of the transmission grid must transmit power for those customers who are free to choose their suppliers. The terms and conditions of such transmission, even if not directly regulated, would be subject to the competition law.

** May be changed in the near future.

Table 4
Indicators of Regulatory Status (continued)

1. What is the ownership/management relationship between the transmission grid and generation?
2. Is the owner of the transmission grid obligated to transmit power for third parties?
3. What is the price control regime for those prices which are controlled?
4. Is there an independent regulator?
5. Is the sector subject to the general competition law?

Country or State	Answer 1	Answer 2	Answer 3	Answer 4	Answer 5
New Zealand	transmission and generation separate, although transmission and almost all generation are state-owned.	yes	information disclosure requirements only	no	yes
Norway	transmission and generation separate, although transmission and some generation are state-owned.	yes	rate-of-return (grid)	yes	yes
Spain*	no, generators forbidden to own more than 30 % of transmission company	yes	costs reimbursed	yes, attached to Min. Industry and Energy	
Sweden*	transmission and generation are separate; transmission is state-owned; some generation is state-owned, other privately owned	yes	price must be cost-based and non-discriminatory; are developing price ceilings complemented by yardstick regulation	yes	yes
United Kingdom	no, forbidden	yes	RPI-x for monopoly parts	yes	yes
United States	options under review to separate ownership and control of the grid	yes	cost of service or price/revenue caps	yes	yes

* Under the Directive on Common Rules for the Internal Market in Electricity, the owner of the transmission grid must transmit power for those customers who are free to choose their suppliers. The terms and conditions of such transmission, even if not directly regulated, would be subject to the competition law.

** May be changed in the near future.

EU Directive on Electricity Liberalisation

The Council of the European Union adopted, on 19 December 1996, a directive on the internal market for electricity. Member States must (with some limited exceptions) implement the directive within two years. The directive concerns access to the grid, mechanisms for entry into power generation and access by some end-users to alternative EU power generators or suppliers.

Three possible access procedures are allowed. Member States can opt for a regulated third party access regime, under which access tariffs are set by regulation. The negotiated third party access system requires publication of indicative negotiated access tariffs. The single-buyer system enables those end-users who are provided choice to arbitrage price differences between "their" supplier and other EU suppliers. Such customers remain entirely a customer of "their" supplier — with the same tariffs, same product offer, etc. — but with the opportunity to receive payments through arbitrage (This could, therefore, be viewed less as an access regime and more as a mechanism to permit financial transactions to arbitrage price differences).

Under the directive, there are two mechanisms for entering the power generation business. Under the licensing option, any company fulfilling basic requirements would be granted a license, so capacity increases would be determined by the market. Under the invitation-to-tender system, the monopoly invites EU companies to tender to build, operate and sell electric power to the monopolist at the price specified in the tender. Under this system, the monopolist determines capacity augmentation according to its central plan; competition in the generation market occurs only at the initial, tendering stage. Independent power producers and autoproducers must be able to obtain a license in Member States which have opted for the tendering system.

The EU Directive sets out a minimum requirement for power sector liberalisation across the European Union. Individual countries can go — and some have gone — further. The Directive provides for a phased, partial opening of the internal market for electric power. By 1999, all customers with final consumption larger than 100 GWh per annum must be free to buy from alternative (domestic or EU foreign) suppliers. Examples of customers who would use more than 100 GWh per annum are automakers, glassworks and chemical plants. For end users smaller than 100 GWh, the market will be partially opened in three steps, in 1999, 2000 and 2003. The calculation of the minimum size of user who is free to choose a supplier is rather complex. For 1999, for example, 40 GWh is the "reference size" of user: The Commission will calculate the percentage of total usage that is accounted for by users of size 40 GWh or more (For 40 GWh, this average is expected to be 23 per cent). In each Member State, those largest users who together account for this average percentage must be free to choose their own suppliers. As the structure of demand differs from one Member State to another, the minimum size of user who is free to choose its own supplier will vary from Member State to Member State, but the percentage of total usage that is subject to liberalisation — absent any additional liberalisation — will be the same in each Member State. For 2000, the "reference size" is 20 GWh (estimated today to constitute about 28 per cent of total usage) and for 2003 the "reference size" is 9 Gwh today.[14]

This type of phased opening may produce interesting dynamic effects. Since users of the same size may be subject to very different rules in the purchase of electricity, if liberalisation does indeed result in substantial price decreases, firms that compete in a downstream "product market" may well pay very different prices for electricity. To the extent that this has important effects on overall profitability, users in less liberalised Member States may exert pressure for greater domestic liberalisation.

---

14. Expressed differently, where $F( )$ is the cumulative share of total usage, r is the "reference size", and i is an index for Member States, $i = 1, 2, ..., 15$, define x so that $x = 1/15 * \Sigma_{i=1}^{15} [1 - F_i(r)]$. For each Member State, there is a size of user m_i which satisfies the condition, $1 - F_i(m_i) = x$. Each Member State i must permit all users of size larger than m_i to choose their own suppliers or, alternatively, Member States must permit all users larger than the "reference size" plus a set of distributors with total usage d so that $1 - F_i(r) - d = x$ is satisfied, to choose their own suppliers.

Member states may choose to extend this liberalisation to distribution companies. Member States are also free to perform a broader liberalisation than that set out in the Directive. This has already occurred in the trade relationships among the Nordic countries. The Directive explicitly states that the EU competition rules continue to apply to the electricity sector.

REGULATORY REFORM: KEY ISSUES

Policy Objectives

It is very important to understand the reasons for regulation, both in the past and in the present. Regulation of the power sector, in various forms and using various mechanisms, was ubiquitous and is still the rule in a majority of countries. Regulation is imposed to meet a number of often conflicting objectives. The resolution of these conflicts is a difficult aspect of reform. The issue may also be presented in the following way: what are liberalised markets capable of delivering? This test needs to be vigorously applied across the range of policy objectives which governments set themselves.

What are the key policy objectives in the power sector? It is helpful to divide these conceptually into categories. The first category consists of objectives which are not being met effectively in the current situation, pre-reform. The most important here is the economic efficiency of the power sector and, hence, its contribution to the wider performance of economies. The second category includes objectives which are being met at present but perhaps at disproportionate cost. Security of supply comes under this heading.

There are objectives which straddle these categories. Market reforms may lead to better handling of environmental concerns, but there are also concerns about the possible impact of reforms. Social objectives such as help to rural areas or to disadvantaged consumers are also mixed into this framework — it is not yet fully clear what markets can deliver (without ongoing regulation).

To summarise, the key policy objectives for the energy sector are:
- Economic efficiency.
- Security of supply.

- Environmental performance.
- Social objectives (including universal service).

There is little doubt that the driver in the current wave of regulatory reform is economic efficiency. Not only must reform deliver on this key objective, but it must also deliver — or continue to deliver — on the rest.

In approaching the issue of regulatory reform, governments therefore need to be clear about the nature of their objectives. But it is just as important to be clear about the potential conflicts, and about the optimal tools or methods for reaching various objectives.

To illustrate the challenge of balancing objectives, the issue of subsidies and cross subsidies is a good example. A cross subsidy occurs when one consumer or consumer group is supplied below cost, whereas the price to others is raised above cost in order to finance this behaviour. Cross subsidies between industrial and residential consumers and between rural and urban customers are widespread. There will not be optimal economic efficiency in a liberalised power market if such subsidies are allowed to remain. It is fundamental to economic efficiency to allow prices to be set through the interplay of supply and demand, without the imposition of distorting rules.

Governments therefore have a choice of whether or not to continue with such rules. If they do, it becomes important to ensure maximum transparency or to find other ways of meeting the underlying objectives. This raises the question of whether these other ways like, for instance, taxation could themselves have a more negative effect on the power market than a subsidy mechanism. Finally, governments need to consider, on a regular basis, whether there remains a need for direct intervention, because it may well be that a liberalised market — though perhaps only in the longer run — will deliver on some policy objectives automatically and without rules.

Industry Structure

The starting point for reform is crucial. There is a need, in some countries, to consider whether parts of the power sector need some consolidation in order to exploit economies of scale in an increasingly international competitive environment. But for most countries the issue is whether to break up a sector which is too concentrated.

Countries need to consider different forms of disaggregation. It can be either vertical or horizontal, or both. Horizontal disaggregation will increase the number of entities active at one level of the industry. Vertical disaggregation will break up the supply chain, through the separation of generation, transmission, distribution, and supply.

Changing the mostly vertical relationship between generation and the transmission grid, and in the vertical relationship between supply and distribution, as well as the horizontal disaggregation of generation, are very important reform issues for any country. However, whether vertical separation is necessary depends on the model of competition chosen. Vertical separation means that some economies of vertical integration will be lost, so the market might have a tendency to gravitate back to some form of integration.

Generation is potentially competitive. Transmission and distribution are still considered to be natural monopolies (though could be owned and used by a number of parties). Supply is also potentially competitive. In order to fulfil the potential for competition in generation, however, some mechanism must be found to ensure non-discriminatory access to the transmission grid by generators and suppliers. That is, some mechanism must eliminate the incentives and the capacity to favour generators with ties to the transmission system. One way to reduce incentives for discrimination is to require separate ownership. In the past, there was concern that generators and the transmission grid would not be able to co-ordinate and plan adequately if they were held under separate ownership or management. However, reformers in the United Kingdom, the state of Victoria and experience with independent power producers elsewhere have found effective mechanisms for the co-ordination of generation and transmission under separate ownership or management.

In countries where the generation and supply functions are highly concentrated, horizontal separation of generation among different entities is a necessary step for competition to develop. It is very important to introduce sufficient competition at the outset, and along all steps of the merit order (*i.e.*, baseload, midload and peak load plants). For a power sector the size of the United Kingdom electricity supply industry, a minimum of five generators had been suggested before privatisation. However, the results do not depend solely on market structure but also on the relevant regulations — including rules for transmission pricing and explicit permission for distribution companies and end-users to contract with generators — and potential for entry. Separation of supply from distribution allows competition to develop in supply.

The nature of the disaggregation is also very important. Vertical separation need not mean full structural separation, with the assets divided up among several newly-formed, legal entities. In the United Kingdom and in the state of Victoria, Australia, generation and transmission have no common ownership, management, control or operations. In Norway, New Zealand, and Sweden, the ultimate owner of both the transmission grid and generation (in Sweden, of some generation) remains in the public sector, but the two parts have been corporatised separately, meaning that there is no common management nor day-to-day control. This arrangement can eliminate incentives to discriminate among generators.

Another approach is functional unbundling, where investors are allowed to enjoy revenue streams from generation and transmission, but where the operation of the grid is in the hands of strictly separate entities, so as to guarantee non-discriminatory grid access. This type of vertical separation has been chosen in

California. In this system, an Independent System Operator, who has no position in the market nor any economic interest in any load or generation, is responsible for short-term co-ordination (such as day-ahead scheduling and hourly re-dispatch), prices for use of the transmission grid (which are to ensure incentives consistent with a competitive market and least-cost use of the transmission grid), and administers a system of tradable transmission congestion contracts (California Public Utility Commission Decision 95-12-063, Part I).

Another, much weaker, form of vertical separation is the unbundling of accounts, whereby the accounts of the different businesses which make up the company are ring-fenced. In theory, accounting separation forces cross subsidies into the open, as the costs and revenues which legitimately accrue to a particular business must be identified. It should, in theory at least, eliminate the ability of incumbent utilities to discriminate in favour of themselves and against competitors in charges for transmission services.

In practice, however, it is very difficult to ensure that accounts are properly unbundled. The process requires complete transparency on the part of the company so that competitors, as well as the regulator, can clearly judge what is going on. The regulator in practice must go into considerable detail in order to satisfy himself that the arrangements are in order. The allocation of joint cash and revenues, as noted, is another problem. In addition, if there is not separate management and independent managerial incentives, then the opportunity and incentives to operate the businesses in an integrated manner, or to discriminate against competitors, would remain. Finally, if the businesses are operated with a common workforce or information system, the opportunity for discriminatory access to commercially valuable information remains.

In its 1996 Order 888, which opens the US wholesale power market to competition, the Federal Energy Regulatory Commission (FERC) requires fully integrated utilities to adhere to a so-called "comparability standard", which means that utilities have to charge themselves for transmission services what they charge others. Of course, the incentives to charge high prices both internally and externally, recouping through higher profits in the non-competitive activity remain, when there is no control over overall profitability or access price. Separation of accounts is also provided for in the EU Directive.

Accounting separation may be the only route for some countries because of issues of ownership and legal status which prevent a move to full structural separation. However, this approach needs to be applied very rigorously if it is to have the desired effect of prompting competition.

Another issue in restructuring which is of potentially great significance is the handling of the supply function. The function may exist independently of the infrastructure elements of the sector (generation, transmission and distribution) with suppliers having no stake in these other elements. The evolution of the supply function is linked to long-term investment and security of supply.

The handling of the distribution part of the sector also needs careful consideration — whether to aim for direct competition for end consumers, or to adopt a model which acknowledges the elements of natural (geographical) monopoly in the sector and seeks to apply competitive pressure through franchising. Results of franchising in other very diverse industries are mixed, and further analysis is needed of the best way forward for electricity.

Ownership

As with structure, ownership is a fundamental issue to be considered in regulatory reform.

Three broad ways in which the relationship between the industry and the State can change are privatisation, corporatisation and corporatisation with incentives. Privatisation means the transfer of assets from the State sector into the private sector, and may be carried out through a stock market flotation or through private sale. "Corporatisation" means financial separation so that financial and asset transfers between the State and the corporatised entity are at arms length and transparent. Corporatisation *per se*, while providing the corporatised entity with greater flexibility and the State with the opportunity to have more explicit performance standards, does not go far towards providing the opportunity or incentives to behave efficiently. For example, transfers at non-market terms can still be made from the State to the entity, or the State can increase the transfers to itself to match exactly any increase in "profits". Corporatisation is, however, sometimes a prelude to privatisation.

Since corporatisation *per se* does not provide much incentive to behave efficiently or competitively, additional incentives may be needed to achieve an efficient outcome. The incentive mechanisms that may go with corporatisation can take several forms including: restrictions on transfers, that is, a "hard budget constraint", a market test for loans, and the refusal by the State to be the lender of last resort; the choice of management through a State-mediated "market" for corporate control; and compensation of management based on contracts with provisions to encourage managers to behave commercially. Further, the State might introduce competition in potentially competitive activities, either among State-owned corporatised entities with contracts with the State that provide incentives to compete, or competition with private entities. Corporatisation needs to be coupled with a mechanism that gives the corporatised entity incentives to increase internal efficiency and to charge efficient prices (subject to meeting transparent, well-specified obligations, such as providing electric power to low income households at specified below-market rates).

Just one dimension, the initial choice of managers, illustrates the possible variations. In New Zealand, many managers came from outside the old organisation and were employed under contracts with performance incentives (Culy, Read and Wright 1996, p. 354). In Victoria, all but two CEOs came from outside the old structure.

In the United Kingdom, by contrast, management largely remained in place during corporatisation.

The starting point for a critical analysis of these various ownership forms is the test of economic efficiency. Numerous studies have been undertaken to explore whether private companies work more efficiently than public ones. This needs to be considered both for the short and the longer term.

For the short term, most studies of IEA countries conclude that ownership alone is not of overwhelming importance for power sector performance.[15] The more important determinants seem to be subjecting potentially competitive parts to more competition and increasing the quality of regulation including corporatisation with incentives. For example, Pollitt examined 768 power plants in 14 countries in 1989, which together account for 40 per cent of world thermal energy. He found that private firms are on average more technically efficient than public firms, by 1 to 3 per cent. In examining the 164 base-load plants for which input price data were available, Pollitt found that private plants were on average more cost efficient than public plants, by about 5 per cent, depending on the methodology used (Pollitt 1994, cited in Gilbert, Kahn and Newbery, pp. 7-8). Despite the relationship between the *averages*, some efficient State-owned utilities were found to be more efficient than private ones.

The long run is different. Long term efficiency tends to be higher in privately-owned utilities than in state-owned ones. One study carried out in Sweden, for example, found that labour productivity in privately-owned utilities remained high, whereas it deteriorated considerably over the course of two decades in state-owned companies.[16] This is of special importance, because long-term

---

15. See e.g. Faere, R. Grosskopt, S. and Logan, J, "The relative performance of publicly-owned and privately-owned electric utilities", Journal of Public Economics, vol. 26, 1985, pp. 89-106; or Atkinson, S.E. and Halvorsen, R. "The relative efficiency of public and private firms in a regulated environment: The case of United States electric utilities", Journal of Public Economics, vo. 29, 1986, pp. 281-294.

16. Kumbhakar, Subal C. and Hjalmarsson, Lennart, "Relative performance of public and private ownership in Swedish electricity retail distribution, 1970-1990", Research Memorandum No. 202, University of Texas at Austin/Goteburg University, August 1994.

efficiency gains, essentially a sustained effort to minimise cost, are better attained by private utilities. It is perhaps not surprising because the key test for sustaining efficiency in market players is whether they are allowed to fail. Only full privatisation will give full play to this strong incentive to succeed.

Corporatisation therefore needs to be approached cautiously. It may not, in the longer term, deliver *sustained* benefits. But it can be a helpful intermediate step to privatisation and, in itself, especially with the right incentives, can achieve much. In some countries, privatisation is very difficult, requiring constitutional changes. In Norway, for example, there is a long tradition of public ownership of natural resources (more than 99 per cent of Norwegian power generation is hydro) and infrastructure activities are traditionally performed by public authorities. It probably would not have been politically acceptable to privatise the power sector. This is why both Statkraft SF and Statnett SF are *statsforetak*, a form of state enterprise that has an obligation to operate on commercial terms and which is relatively independent of government. Sweden has a similar structure.

By contrast, in both the United Kingdom and the state of Victoria privatisation was considered to be a key, necessary part of the reform.[17]

Given the nature of assets in the power sector, if governments cannot credibly commit to a regulatory policy free of influence by competitors or undue political influence, or do not have a well-functioning judicial system, they may have no choice but to have their power sector under public ownership, as private investment may be deterred. In this case, however, corporatisation with incentives would seem to provide substantial benefits, although there remains the continued risk of political interference.

---

17. *Victoria was explicitly seen as engaged in global competition for private investment and it was considered important, for public policy, for such investment to be efficiently directed.*

Models of Competition

Competition in the power sector will not succeed if governments dismantle statutory entry barriers — and leave it at that. Where this approach has been tried — as in the United Kingdom with the 1983 Energy Act that removed the statutory entry barrier established by the 1909 Electric Lighting Act — the market response was negligible or nil. A central issue in power sector liberalisation is the fact that a key part of the sector, transmission and, over a specified geographic area, distribution is currently a monopoly and will continue as a monopoly for the foreseeable future. It is cheaper for a single efficient facility to provide these services than for two or more to do so. It may be possible, nonetheless, to formulate ownership and management in such a way as to permit competition in use of the unique facility. In order for effective competition to develop, non-discriminatory access to the grid needs to be secured.

Two main options to achieve this have been developed so far: the "grid access" model, and the "competitive pool" model.

■ The Grid Access Model

Under the grid access model, the owner of the grid must allow competitors to use it, on non-discriminatory terms and prices; the grid owner must not discriminate in favour of itself. Under this model, vertical separation is not envisaged. Under the several variants of this model, terms and conditions for access to the grid can be determined in different ways: they can be negotiated with market actors negotiating their own terms, or they can be regulated with an independent regulator setting or arbitrating the terms. Some commentators also distinguish between voluntary and mandatory grid access; conceptually, denial of access to the grid is equivalent to setting a very high negotiated price, hence this separate category is not necessary. Regulated grid access is effective because, if the terms are set correctly, it enables those competitors, including entrants, who are more efficient in non-grid activities than the vertically-integrated utility, to enter other activities, predominantly generation. Further, total transaction costs including the cost of prolonged negotiations or litigation are probably lower than for negotiated access pricing. Negotiated grid access is less effective for the promotion of competition or even entry. The vertically integrated incumbent will not, in general, set access terms that permit all more efficient entrants to enter. In setting those terms, the vertically integrated company will take account of the profits it will lose if it allows competitors into generation.

■ The Competitive Pool Model

The competitive pool model is a combination of grid access rules and a competitive spot market for wholesale electricity. It requires vertical separation of generation and transmission and of generation and supply. This is fundamental to the effective operation of this model. There must also be adequate competition in generation to avoid the pool price being set above competitive levels. A certain degree of integration between generation and distribution may be admissible provided certain conditions are met. Competition in generation and supply and regulatory oversight can counterbalance to some extent the negative effects of vertical integration. The grid access rules ensure that competing generators can reach ultimate consumers, whereas the pool is a short term, multilateral market for power exchange.

In jurisdictions that have implemented this model, the pool is usually managed by a distinct entity, who has no economic or managerial interest in generation or transmission. The spot market plays the paramount role in determining which plants are dispatched and which are not. Essentially, the spot market establishes a merit order, except that it is not based on the reported short term marginal cost of generating units, as is the case in more traditional centralised systems, but on price bids. The lowest bidding unit is dispatched first. The highest-bidding unit which is still dispatched determines the system price received by all generators who are operating at any one moment. Most competitive pools feature both an energy price component (per MWh) and a capacity price component (intended as an incentive to long term investment). They also incorporate a wedge between the spot market price, which is paid to generators, and the price charged to buyers, which incorporates payments to those supplying ancillary services.

Competitive pool models of competition have generated futures and options markets based on electric power as the underlying commodity. Unless consumers are willing to pay the pool admission fee and accept the full volatility of pool prices, in short to buy directly from the spot market, financial markets provide a way to off-load risk. Pool prices can be subject to enormous fluctuations: the pool purchase price in England and Wales varies more than four-fold through a daily cycle, and has, over longer time periods, shown variations of a scope of one to a hundred. Depending upon the set-up of the system (whether or not the pool rules allow negative prices),[18] prices can vary between zero and the full value of lost load (VoLL), which has been set at approximately Pounds 2.5/MWh in the United Kingdom and at A$ 5,000/MWh in Victoria. This means that, in principle, price variations can be much larger than the already large observed values.

■ The Single Buyer Variation

These two main types of competition in the power sector show a number of variations in practice. One variation is especially interesting, however. It is the "Single Buyer" model, one of the options countries can choose under the EU Directive. The "Single Buyer" has two principal components. The first is a competitive bidding mechanism for new capacity: an entity separated from the incumbent utility collects bids for tender for new capacity construction and subsequent supply of power when the need arises and chooses the cheapest one. The second component is the

---

18. *In some countries, e.g. Norway, negative prices can occur, and actually have occurred during the summer of 1995. However, most markets with a competitive pool do not allow negative prices to occur.*

possibility to carry out so-called "triangular" transactions. If a client of the incumbent utility wishes to buy power from a competitor, the "Single Buyer" buys the power from the client at source, or at the "border" of his system at his retail price less the transmission price. He then transmits it for the client, and sells it to him at the retail rate.

■ Evaluation of the Models

The grid access model was chosen by the United States for its wholesale deregulation (FERC Order 888), by the European Union for its internal electricity market, and, in their individual reform programmes, by several Canadian provinces, Finland,[19] Germany, Japan, the Netherlands, and Portugal. The competitive pool model has so far been chosen by Australia,[20] Canada (Alberta),[21] New Zealand, Norway, Spain, Sweden, the United Kingdom (England and Wales), and the United States (California).

The choice between these models depends on a number of factors, but among the main determinants are existing structure and ownership patterns. In some cases, it would be impossible (without changes in primary legislation or even of the constitution) to carry out full vertical separation, and thus to introduce the competitive pool model especially where federal governments lack the right to interfere in private entities' ownership rights. This is the case for the United States or Germany. In this sense, it is the longevity of the assets that conditions optimal strategies for power sector reform. A notable observer of reform of the power sector, Professor Newbery, has pointed out that there is an "option value" to some reforms because opportunities for radical reform of the

---

19. In Finland, the transmission and interconnection assets of the previously fully vertically integrated utilities (Imatran Voima Oy (IVO) and Pohjolan Voima Oy (PVO)) were transferred to a new, partially vertically separated transmission company called Suomen Kantaverkko Oy (SKO) in November 1996. The company will start operations in April 1997. See Finnish Ministry of Trade and Industry (ed.): Finnish Energy Review 4/96.

20. In Victoria at present, but the future national electricity market, and reform in other states, will also be based on this model.

21. Alberta does not, however, envisage competition in supply. This means that grid access is limited to the wholesale level.

power sector are rare, a main determinant of the choice of structure should be whether it forecloses future options (Newbery in OECD 1995, p. 240).

Since competitive pool models function best if generation and transmission are separated, they do contain an element of inefficiency, simply because there are significant economies of vertical integration between these two elements, some of which will be lost through separation. However, it is generally assumed that the combined effects of increased productive efficiency, both in the short and long terms, and the greater efficiency in the allocation of resources outweigh this loss of efficiency.

The competitive pool model is, however, likely to promote the greatest short term efficiency. Hard evidence is not yet available, but four factors point into this direction.

First, trading in the pool determines dispatch decisions (subject to transmission constraints). Because the number of competitive transactions is much larger than in simple grid access systems, the pool model permits pricing that better reflects systems cost. Consumers have the choice either to engage in contractual relationships that use the pool price as their reference price, or to take the pool price as it comes, without alleviation of the volatility. The Finnish example shows what can be achieved by a grid access model. In the Finnish Electricity Exchange (EL-EX), standardised bilateral forward contracts are traded, using a powerful computerised model developed on the basis of experience in other commodity markets. However, the number of transactions is still much smaller than in pool systems, partly because the number of participants is small: only three per cent of power sales in Finland are traded in the EL-EX, whereas competitive pools are typically mandatory except for very small generating units. Nearly 100 per cent of power sold is traded in the spot market. Unlike in gas spot markets it matters that the electricity pool should cover as many power sales as possible of the total, because electricity is not storable and all plants have to be dispatched in the merit order in order to minimise cost or maximise efficiency.

The second point is that grid access models cannot guarantee that all power is dispatched throughout the entire market. One of the core requirements of an efficient power market is that plants be dispatched in the cost- minimising merit order throughout the entire market, and that the market be big enough. Demand and supply should be aggregated until the incremental benefits of aggregation fall below the additional transmission cost (losses and grid extension) that this aggregation causes. However, generators and clients in grid access models cannot be prevented from engaging in direct, bilateral, physical power exchanges. While this may be advantageous for the parties engaging in the transaction, it breaks plant away from the cost-minimising merit order, and is thus likely to increase overall system cost. This would leave those consumers who continue to be supplied from the centralised system with higher cost.[22] Going back to the Finnish example, it is the fact that *physical forwards* rather than *financial futures* are traded that induces this inefficiency.

The third factor is the increased transparency that the competitive pool provides. The pool price is information that can be observed by everybody, market participants and potential entrants alike. Potential entrants and incumbents thus obtain information on which to base their entry and investment decisions.

The fourth factor is that, in the grid access model, an incompletely separated company retains the incentive, and may well have the ability, to circumvent non-discrimination rules, and so disadvantage its potential rivals in ways that regulators cannot effectively detect and prevent. For example, if the transmission grid is not operated by a fully independent system operator, the incumbent could discriminate against competitors on the grounds of lacking or overloaded transmission capacity, without the regulator being able to exercise effective oversight. Similar problems may arise with respect to the cost of and time required to connect competitors to the grid.

---

22. For a more comprehensive discussion regarding the efficiency benefits of a competitive pool, see e.g., Hogan, W.W. "An efficient bilateral market needs a pool", presentation given at California Public Utilities Commission Hearing, San Francisco, 4 August 1994.

Another issue for further consideration in evaluating the competitive pool model relates to the question of long term security of supply. In a competitive market an equilibrium between supply and demand should theoretically be struck which reflects both short and long term energy security concerns; in the short term the ability to cover demand at all times; in the long term, sufficient capacity investment. Price signals should trigger the necessary decisions from market participants. The issue is that the incentives for pool prices to be set to reflect long term security of supply needs, i.e., price signals for long term investment, may come relatively late.

This brings to the fore the potentially pivotal role of suppliers, or service providers, who make the wholesale purchases on behalf of end customers. These service providers are not necessarily involved at all in the actual infrastructure of the power sector, but only provide the service of purchasing electricity to deliver to consumers. They must be enabled to evolve effectively, and the framework established for competition must help them to integrate long as well as short term security considerations. In effect, the service providers may need to make up the consumers' inclination to discount or ignore long term security concerns.

Assessing the comparative efficiency of the "Single Buyer" model is more complex. Firstly, the competitive capacity bidding system only refers to capacity construction, not operation, which will remain in the hands of the independent system operator, who is required to be independent from both the incumbent utility and the single buyer. There will thus be no alteration to dispatch patterns. Whether or not the triangular transactions are carried out as direct, bilateral physical transactions is not clear at the outset; this depends on how the system is designed. It seems likely, however, that "triangular" power imports do not involve dispatch of the foreign plant in the importing system's merit order. Whether this causes efficiency losses depends on how the plant was dispatched before, and in which system it is dispatched most efficiently.

If the "Single Buyer" is set up optimally, so that the incumbent utility, the system operator, and the tendering agency for new capacity are separate entities, and if the price of transmission is set appropriately, and there is no information flow between those entities, this system should result in the same outcome as the grid access model. If this cannot be achieved, the "Single Buyer" would have obvious incentives to discriminate against competitors. Further clarification is needed on how countries intend to establish the "Single Buyer" in practice before judgement can be passed. "Chinese walls" between the Single Buyer's institutions will, however, be difficult to erect and maintain.

It should be noted that centralised power markets have not always performed well on security of supply, occasionally underinvesting (e.g. Italy).

Related Financial Markets

The development of financial markets is a response to structural changes in the power sector. The trading of these financial instruments facilitates the shifting of some types of risk from those for whom exposure to risk is particularly costly onto those, perhaps not even participants in the power sector, who are willing to reduce or to bear this risk at least cost.

The power market is subject to a variety of risks, among them changes in fuel prices, changes in inflation and interest rates, short-term and long-term demand shifts, weather, equipment failures, and regulatory and political risk. Under a regulatory regime where utilities' prices are set so that their revenues cover costs, at least in the absence of high inflation and high interest rates, much of the risk is passed from the electric utilities onto end-users. For example, where utilities are permitted to pass through all changes in the price of fuel to end users, they avoid exposure to fuel price risk. Electric utilities also have, historically, reduced their exposure to fuel price fluctuations through trading in gas or petroleum futures markets. Other risks, such as the size of long-term demand, are passed onto end-users in the form of unreliable or low quality electric power or higher prices to pay for the cost of unused excess capacity. At the same time, under cost-plus regulation, the prices offered end-users were set, except for fuel adjustment clauses, for relatively long terms and short-term fluctuations in electricity demand were correlated with fluctuations in quantity of fuel used.

As the power sector is dis-integrated, new markets are created and, because the markets receive shocks — daily shifts in demand, etc. — the market prices are volatile. For example, the spot price for electricity in Norway rose dramatically after a cold, dry winter left the lakes of this 99 per cent hydro-powered system at low levels. In the past, the hourly variations in marginal cost of supply were borne by the power sector. The year-to-year variations of the Norwegian system would also have been borne by the power sector, which in other years would have benefited from wet weather and lower costs. But after dis-integration, the variations in marginal cost of supply are reflected in the spot market price, where it is felt by all market participants who pay spot prices. The purpose of the changes in the risk-allocation mechanism is not to eliminate risk — human and economic activity will continue to vary in unexpected ways — but rather to shift the risk onto those who can reduce it, or are willing to bear it, at the lowest price.

Bilateral contracts can provide some risk shifting, as illustrated in the example below of a "contract for differences". A company may write a unique instrument for its particular situation, or instruments might be standardised and traded in markets. Liquid markets for financial instruments based on electricity provide greater opportunities for risk-shifting because one's exposure to risk can be continuously changed, More risk-averse persons can more cheaply shed risk onto the less risk-averse, whether or not these persons are participants in the power sector. For example, entry by independent power producers in the United Kingdom was facilitated by two sets of long-term bilateral contracts. Under a contract to sell electricity for a large part of the output of the

Independent Power Producers (IPP), the regional electricity company (which typically also had an equity interest in the IPP) would reduce the IPP's demand risk. Under a take-or-pay gas purchase contract covering most of the IPP's fuel requirements, an important cost risk for the IPP was reduced.

In some jurisdictions that have established a spot market for power, markets for financial instruments based on the spot price have also been established. These markets permit the price risk to be shifted. Through such markets, an electricity buyer or seller can, for a price, reduce her exposure to the price volatility in the spot market. For example, one can use these markets to form a price floor or price ceiling. Unlike some other options based on commodities, these options are generally settled for cash. Generally the electric power is not actually delivered at settlement. These instruments may in principle cover price risk (the change in the spot or pool price) and basis risk (change in the difference between two prices, such as the price of gas and the price of electric power), among other sorts of risk.

One such market, established in early 1996, is the New York Mercantile Exchange's (NYMEX) Electricity Futures and Options Market. This market has a standardised trading unit (a specified number of megawatt hours, delivered at a specified rate over a specified period of time), a limited number of possible strike prices and of trading months, and other contract specifications that facilitate secondary trading. Nord Pool and EL-EX Electricity Exchange provide, respectively, financial futures trading and physical futures trading for electric power in Norway, Sweden, and Finland. One notable risk that cannot be hedged with contracts traded in these markets is locational risk, the unpredictable changes in the difference between the price at the trading location (specified in the financial instrument) and the location where the trader has physical delivery or receiving obligations. In electric power, these unpredictable changes may be due, for example, to varying transmission capacity.

Box 4

Contracts for Differences:
An Illustration of Spot Market Price Risk Reduction

The contract specifies a strike price, a quantity of electric power, a time and a rule for payments. In this example, the rule is: If the pool price is higher than the strike price at that time, the Generator pays the Supplier the pool price minus the strike price; if the pool price is lower than the strike price at that time, then Supplier pays Generator the strike price minus the pool price. Assume that the pool price, say 11, is higher than the strike price, say 10. Then the Generator pays the Supplier 1. The Generator receives 11 from its sales of electric power into the pool; so the Generator gets a total unit revenue of 10 (11 from the pool minus the amount, 1, that was paid to the Supplier) and Supplier pays a total unit price of 10 (pays 11 to the pool and gets a payment of 1 from Generator). By this contract, both Generator and Supplier completely cover the risk of price volatility in the pool; they are guaranteed to be paid and to pay respectively, a price of 10, for the specified quantity and time.

An alternative contract might have the rule: If the pool price is higher than the strike price at that time, then Generator pays the Supplier the pool price minus the strike: if the pool price is lower than the strike price at that time, then there is no payment. The contract effectively sets a maximum price the Supplier must pay for the specified quantity of electricity at that time. But the contract does not completely protect Supplier from price volatility above the strike price: CfDs may be traded and changes in expectations about the pool price are reflected in changes in the price of the CfD owned by the Supplier.

These financial instruments and markets play a key role in the markets for electric power. In the United Kingdom, for example, "contracts for differences" (CfD) covered 80 per cent of sales (by volume) to non-franchise customers in 1995/96. While CfDs vary significantly in terms, an illustrative example is provided in Box 4 (p. 56).

Regulatory Structure

In many countries, regulation has been carried out within government, typically the Ministry responsible for the power sector. Ownership changes, the associated restructuring and changes in regulations require a reappraisal of the most effective regulatory mechanism to oversee and apply the rules. Indeed this needs to be considered as early in the reform process as possible because the quality of regulation has a critical impact on the effectiveness of reforms. There is little point embarking on reforms to give more independence to market players if the regulatory mechanism continues to result in micro-management and/or direct interference with the decision-making process within companies.

The most important attribute of effective regulation is independence. This, at the very least, means independence from the companies that are being regulated. The regulator should also be independent from day-to-day political control of government itself (as has happened in the United Kingdom with the establishment of OFFER at arm's length from the Department of Trade and Industry). However, this does raise some potentially difficult issues about accountability of the independent regulator. But at the same time it removes difficult issues about direct political interference and lack of neutrality and transparency, which can discourage investment in the sector as well as economically efficient behaviour. The United States has sought to resolve this problem through the establishment of a Commission of political or elected appointees to whom the regulator is answerable (FERC).

Whichever model is chosen, an independent regulator provides some assurance to market participants, especially new entrants, that regulatory rules will be oriented towards the efficiency and performance of the sector. It also engenders confidence that rules will be applied and enforced in a way which is non-discriminatory, transparent, consistent, stable and without day-to-day interference from government. In particular, "the same rules for everyone" is an objective which is best applied from a position of independence.

While sector-specific regulatory authorities require specific knowledge of the sector, it is important for the general competition law to apply to it, excepting only those elements that are covered by sector-specific rules. Countries need to consider the structure for ensuring that these rules — general and sector-specific — are applied to best effect. If they opt for a general competition authority approach (i.e., no sector-specific regulator) it is important that this competition authority should have the necessary expertise to deal effectively with the power sector and its complexities.

Pricing: the Transmission Grid

No matter how competitive generation and supply are reorganised, the remaining natural monopoly elements, essentially the transmission grid require special regulatory attention if optimum economic efficiency is to be achieved.

The introduction of competition in generation and supply puts particular pressure on the regulation of transmission pricing, because this factor critically determines the effectiveness of competition in the other parts of the supply chain. The terms of access to the transmission grid are fundamental to the development of competition in those other parts. The situation is more complex than in, for example, telecommunications, which has a similar issue of pricing access to the telecommunications network. The transmission grid enables various economies to be exploited: economies of scale in generating plant, economies in system reliability and system-wide economies of scale and scope via the bundling of differing customers loads and dispatching a portfolio of power plants in a cost-minimising merit order. The difficulty lies in how to price efficiently the costs associated with investment in maintenance and use of the grid. Electricity networks raise two sets of fundamental and interdependent issues: the first, technical; the second, economic.

The most important technical issue is the phenomenon of loop flows. There are other technical features that complicate transmission pricing, such as voltage limitations at the nodes in conjunction with reactive power "flows". Loop flows arise from a law of physics, namely that electricity travels along the path of least resistance — in other words, not along a pre-determined path which respects the terms of a contract for its supply. In meshed networks, this means that power may flow through a multitude of parallel paths according to grid status, which may itself change from one moment to another, and which is influenced by all users of the grid. Loop flows thus constitute a grid externality. Using an example from North America, power deliveries between Canadian generators and the New York Power Pool may cause loop flows going as far south as Ohio and Kentucky. In order to avoid loading of certain power lines beyond their thermal capacity, some lines may not be used even if the amount of power shipped increases.

The economic issue is how to price transmission in order to reflect transmission costs and grid externalities correctly. In a highly simplified approach, transmission costs can be separated into three categories. These are the cost of building and maintaining transmission capacity, the cost of marginal losses (losses of power as it is transported) and congestion costs. In addition, grid connection itself may generate costs (the technical costs of reinforcing the infrastructure to meet the needs of new entrants).

Pricing mechanisms for transmission services have evolved alongside the development of competition. Early approaches were based on transmission rights, whereby one utility would obtain the incumbent grid owner's permission to use a certain amount of his grid capacity against remuneration. These transmission rights could be firm or interruptible.

The pricing mechanisms developed for this approach were often not very sophisticated. They included "postage stamp" transmission tariffs, zonal "postage stamp" methods, and Megawatt-kilometre pricing. The three approaches vary in the degree to which they reflect the spatial dimension of electricity transmission. "Postage stamp" rates are the least sophisticated approach and are based on simple division of total network cost by total connected load, much as a real stamp does when a letter is sent. This yields a price per MW transported that is based on the premise that the network provides the same service to all users, and that there is no need to allocate cost more precisely. It is so remote from the underlying cost structure of the transmission grid that it is clearly an inferior solution. Zonal "postage stamps" reflect the spatial dimension somewhat better, in that they separate the whole grid into smaller zones. Transmission within each zone is cheaper than transmission across two or more zones. This pricing mechanism can be further differentiated according to voltage, and is already more cost-reflective than the undifferentiated "postal stamp". The Megawatt-kilometre method is based on the assumption that the length of the transmission route and the amount of power transmitted provide a reasonable proxy for transmission cost. This is based on the recognition that marginal losses are related to distance.

All three methods are, however, far removed from the underlying technical and economic characteristics of grid operation. More complex, but also more appropriate pricing methods have been developed in markets with more competition, such as the United Kingdom, where the cost components are priced independently. The most sophisticated transmission pricing method is known as nodal pricing or locational spot pricing.[23] Much as in the transportation of other goods, it states that the price at any given point A in the network should equal the price at another point B plus the cost of

---

23. This pricing mechanism was developed by Bohn, R.E., Caramanis, M., and Schweppe, F.C., in: Optimal Pricing in Electrical Networks over Space and Time. In: Rand Journal of Economics, Vol. 18, No. 3, 1984. It has recently been recommended for use in real power systems by Hogan. See e.g.: Hogan, W.W.: Contract Networks for Electric Power Transmission. In: Journal of Regulatory Economics, pp. 211-42, 1992.

transportation from A to B. Failing this, arbitrage would take place; the good from point B would be shipped to the overpriced point A, which would eventually depress the price at A to the optimal level. In the presence of competition, the price at each location or "node" would be equal to marginal production and transportation cost (transportation cost can, in the case of electricity, be thought of as marginal losses).

However, nodal pricing does not adequately take account of all the complexities of the grid. Because of the externalities of transmission such as the loop flow phenomenon, nodal pricing can lead to counter-intuitive and sub-optimal investment and operation decisions, which may in turn lead to "wrong" geographical location of new power plants and grid extension, particularly if trading is based on a network of contracts.[24] Nodal pricing can also result in prices at the "sending" node, *i.e.* the seller's price, being higher than at the "receiving" node, *i.e.* the buyer's price. In this case, under normal market conditions, there would not be a transaction. In practice, an independent system operator takes care of these externalities.

No fully satisfactory solution for transmission grid pricing has been found yet. However, some recent technological developments could allow much better control of electricity flows in the grid. High-power switches called thyristors,[25] which can switch off a current at very high speed as it moves through the grid, can bring actual electricity flows more in line with the contractual path specified between consumers and producers. It has other benefits, such as allowing loading of transmission lines much closer to capacity, thereby immediately increasing overall grid capacity. Recent developments in semi-conductor technology go beyond this performance. Once this equipment has reached market maturity, it will bring the power grid much closer to other infra-

---

24. See Oren, S., Spiller, P., Varaiya, P., and Wu, F.: *Nodal Prices and Transmission Rights: A Critical Appraisal.* In: The Electricity Journal, Vol. 8, No. 3, April 1995.
25. See e.g. Stahlkopf, K.: *The Second Silicon Revolution.* In: Einhorn, M., and Siddiqi, R.: Electricity Transmission Pricing and Technology. Boston, Dordrecht and London, 1996.

structure networks, and will allow some simplification of the very intricate pricing issues. This is crucial, as recognition grows that transmission lies at the heart of competition in the power market. As long as cost cannot be allocated correctly, not only will the system deviate from optimal performance but the playing field for competition itself may be skewed.

Pricing: End Users

In non-competitive power sectors governments are concerned about the pricing behaviour of monopoly entities (from the end user's perspective). There must be a requirement or incentive to price closer to cost and eliminate monopoly rent. In power markets that are being opened up to competition there remains a concern about captive, mainly residential consumers whom competition does not directly reach and, more generally, about the incentives to offer lower prices. These concerns reflect the fact that competition is still evolving and it may be that price regulation will become unnecessary in due course. However, in the power sector — unlike some other utilities — it is not certain whether full competition across the whole supply chain will ever be possible. Transmission seems set to remain a natural monopoly for the foreseeable future — and therefore there may be an ongoing requirement for price controls of some kind.

It is important to distinguish two distinct categories of price regulation: regulation of price structures and control of price levels. As regards price structures, it is fairly well accepted that electricity price "menus" are efficient only if they contain all of the following:

- **Peak-load pricing.** Since electrical load, and system cost, vary in daily and seasonal patterns, utilities have increasingly charged time-of-use rates. The larger the consumers, the more closely pricing patterns reflect system cost and its sometimes erratic developments.

- **Multi-part tariffs.** If end-user rates are to reflect cost appropriately, cost elements which are customer-related but do not vary with kWh consumption need to be priced as a fixed fee. For very small users, it can even be efficient to cover some of the consumption- related cost via that fixed fee.

- **Interruptible service pricing.** Numerous mechanisms have been developed to reflect consumers' preferences for reliability in their prices. They take account of the randomness of demand fluctuations and supply problems, and generally attribute much lower prices to consumers who are willing to put up with limited supply interruptions.

Peak-load and interruptible-service pricing provide incentives for users to shift demand away from peak periods, thus reducing the need for expensive capacity and lowering total cost.

There are two main types of control of price levels: rate of return (ROR) regulation and price capping. ROR regulation is the standard form of utility regulation in the United States, where it is carried out by independent Public Utilities Commissions in the states. It sets a rate of return on capital employed for the industry, which is assessed primarily on the basis of the capital required to produce and supply electricity. Price capping sets limits on price increases linked to the rate of inflation, to yield stable real prices, reduced by the regulator's assessment of possible productivity increases (X), and increased again by allowances for fuel cost increases (Y). This yields the formula for allowed annual price increases RPI-X+Y. This rule is usually in place for a pre-announced length of time, such as five years, and then reviewed for possible revision of the value of X or any sub-caps; there are often also sub-caps to limit flexibility in the structure prices. It was invented in the United Kingdom and is the main approach used in that country. Yardstick regulation consists of comparing a utility's rates with those of several comparable utilities. If one utility is more efficient than others, it keeps more profits; if less efficient, its prices will not be increased or reduced. Some of the Nordic countries emphasise yardstick regulation.

ROR regulation has long been recognised as containing some adverse incentives, in particular the incentive to overinvest in capital assets or "gold plating". It is difficult for the regulator to have enough information on the company to set the ROR at the most efficient level. However, the United States approach is sophisticated, involving not just the assessment of capital required to produce and supply electricity (the rate base) but also the determination of a fair rate of return on this rate base. The fair ROR is based in inter-industry comparison and allows cost components thought to be largely out of the utility's control, such as fuel cost, to be passed through.

Price capping has some advantages over ROR regulation, because it acknowledges that the major source of a monopoly's inefficiency may be a failure to reduce costs rather than to charge excess prices and because it provides increased incentives for efficiency improvements which the regulator cannot otherwise identify or enforce. However, if the regulator assesses X and Y incorrectly, he may force companies' prices below cost, or may leave a part of the monopoly profits in place. The latter option may not be a bad thing, because the regulator is bound to notice, at some stage, that he has not set X high, or Y low enough. In that case, it is likely that he will adjust those parameters. This is equivalent to the notion of the regulatory time lag, with attempts to improve efficiency by letting well-performing utilities keep their "excess" profits for a limited amount in time and regulate them away only after a while. This gives utilities an incentive to minimise cost because they can reap benefits from such actions, at least temporarily. However, as with ROR, it is very hard to set the cap, because the regulator needs information which may be hard to come by and the interpretation of that information is also difficult.[26]

Yardstick regulation has been applied to fully vertically integrated utilities and distributors/suppliers, but on its own, it is likely to be

---

26. *One such case actually occurred in the competitive United Kingdom market in 1994, where, after carrying out a review of price controls, the regulator realised that the regional electricity companies (RECs) had gone much further than anticipated in their cost-cutting discipline, and that they were much more profitable.*

the least effective approach. This is due to the tremendous unavoidable cost differences between utilities, especially at the distribution end. Although it is theoretically possible to characterise a benchmark utility via regression analysis, there are rarely enough utilities to reach significant results. Yardstick regulation is therefore best used in combination with other methods.

Subsidies and Cross Subsidies

Regulatory reform of the power sector must also review subsidies and cross-subsidies. Cross-subsidies between industrial and residential consumers have been suspected to be widespread in the past, but are notoriously difficult to prove. Generally speaking, smaller consumers, especially residential and small service consumers, have peakier loads than large industrial consumers, thus cause higher cost, and therefor should be charged higher prices. Thus, a power system that shows lower rates for residential customers than for industry can reasonably be suspected of engaging in internal subsidisation. Another type of cross subsidy occurs between rural and urban consumers if they are charged geographically uniform prices despite the very location sensitive cost of distribution. This type of cross subsidy is easily observable and, indeed, ubiquitous. Governments may have promoted this kind of cross subsidy for social or equity reasons and to ease pressure on already densely populated urban agglomerations.

The English and Welsh system uses a type of cross-subsidy, the Fossil Fuel Levy, currently set at 2.2 per cent (formerly at 10 per cent), which is designed to ensure diversity of electricity generating capacity, and notably to encourage generation by renewables (and, formerly, nuclear energy sources). The tax to pay for the subsidy is levied on sales of certain electricity in a transparent way, and the subsidy is spent to support capacity which would be uneconomic without it. This capacity is determined in a competitive bidding process (the so-called Non-Fossil Fuel Obligation, NFFO). So far, four bidding rounds have been carried out. Given that it is paid by all electricity suppliers through their use of the wires, rather than just end-users, it is unclear among which end-users the incidence of the levy falls (MMC Report on PowerGen plc and Midlands Electricity plc, paras. 3.20-3.22). Other public policy objectives supported by cross subsidies may include aid to low income consumers and support for R&D.

Cross subsidies are therefore present to some degree in probably all power sectors and they exist for a variety of reasons, many of which are linked to governments' underlying policy objectives for the sector. The difficulty with cross subsidies is that they distort the optimum economically efficient and cost-related approach to pricing. They can also involve difficult trade-offs between conflicting public policy objectives. The subsidisation of rural electricity consumers in big, sparsely populated countries such as Australia is thought to destroy niche markets for non-grid renewable electricity supply options so bringing into potential conflict social objectives and the promotion of renewable power generation.

This is not to say that governments should avoid all forms of subsidies and cross subsidies. But they should consider very carefully the mechanisms for subsidisation, having first clearly identified the policy reasons for it and eliminated those which do not support clearly defined objectives. Regulation should also consider the potential conflict between different objectives. They should be aware that subsidies of any kind will introduce some distortion into optimum economic price setting.

Mechanisms should minimise distortion, be fully transparent and avoid discrimination again new market entrants. They might include direct government payment of transparent subsidies (rather than companies themselves making the subsidies between categories of consumer), grid charges, customer service fees, portfolio standards and credits trading mechanisms. Even direct government subsidies, however, come at a cost; the subsidy has to be financed, and nearly all known forms of taxation are ill-suited to promote economic efficiency or distribution of income.

Governments should also regularly review whether a subsidy is still needed. Ideally, subsidies should expire after a pre-determined time and only be extended if explicit action is taken. In particular, governments should be alert to the possibility that the competitive market itself may start to deliver automatically. For example, it may be in companies' interests to develop services for particular customer categories or to provide a universal service.

Cross subsidies applied by companies themselves which do not support governments' public policy objectives should be eliminated where they interfere with competition. In particular, subsidies by vertically integrated utilities across different parts of their business, which disadvantage newcomers to the business, should be eliminated.

General Competition Law, Competitive Neutrality, State Aids

A key starting point in power sector competition is dismantling statutory entry barriers, which have often taken the form of exemptions from general competition law. In the EU, for example, special or exclusive rights may be imposed in the public interest which would otherwise be contrary to the competition provisions of the Treaty of Rome; and the liberalisation legislation is partly aimed at lifting these rights or circumscribing their effect.

The application of general competition law is important. Not only does it remove special rights which may limit market entry, but it also provides a further tool with which to support the evolution of competition, supplementing and, sometimes, instead of the sector specific rules reviewed in the last section. For example, general competition authorities can play a useful role in setting access pricing rules, prosecuting abuse of dominant positions including that practised against new entrants and captive customers, and preventing anticompetitive contracts, mergers and joint ventures. Special competition rules for the sector should be avoided, as this could create uncertainty over which rules apply and distortions of investment decisions.

A summary of the situation for selected countries is provided in Table 4 (p. 32-33).

A number of countries like New Zealand and Finland have chosen a model of "light handed" regulation, so called because it relies on general competition law and mandatory information disclosure rather than on sector-specific regulation. Under the general competition law of those countries, there are usually provisions prohibiting abuse of dominance through excessive pricing.

In Norway the competition authority and the regulator have been directed by their respective ministers divide their labour and responsibility. They have agreed that the competition authority is responsible for competition and that the sector-specific regulatory authority, NVE is responsible for regulation of network activities of the distribution companies. They have further agreed to co-operate in areas of overlapping responsibilities such as access issues and foreign trade in electricity. They exchange information on competition in the markets.

In the United Kingdom, general competition law applies to mergers in the power sector although for a few years there was a transitional arrangement which had the effect of blocking any mergers involving the sector. In Australia, where the competition law applies to the electricity sector as well as to other "network infrastructure" industries, recent amendments to the competition law were made in anticipation of the increased role the competition authorities would have in such industries. An industry code of conduct, the National Electricity Code, has been developed for the proposed competitive electricity market and has been submitted to the Australian Competition and Consumer Commission for authorisation. In Victoria, while there is a transitional arrangement to limit mergers in the sector, mergers and take-overs will be dealt with as under the general Australian competition law after the year 2 000.

There are fundamental differences between general competition law and sector specific regulation. While the general competition law applied to mergers is prospective, the law applied to behaviour deals with a problem after it has arisen rather than anticipating issues with rules which apply regardless of actual behaviour. There is a fundamental difference on where the burden of proof lies, how specific the rules are and the penalties for violating the rules. Therefore, governments need to consider carefully the application of general competition law to open the market, at least in the early stages. New market entrants are particularly vulnerable to the power of established incumbents. There is also the issue of how to deal effectively with captive consumers. Such consumers are unlikely to find it easy or cheap to tackle problems through general competition law and the courts, and it is easier if there are clear rules which their suppliers need to follow.

However, the competitive elements of the market clearly do not need as intrusive an approach as the non-competitive elements, once the market is established, and governments need to keep the arrangements under review. If it is possible to dismantle special rules, this should always be considered. The more rules, the more likelihood of distortion of optimal market decision making.

Another, very important, function of general competition law is the control of mergers, alliances and joint ventures. The economies of vertical integration mean that companies may have a natural incentive to re-integrate, especially vertically. When power sector reforms have sought to disaggregate the industry, as in the competitive pool model of competition, re-integration is a problem. In the competitive pool model, vertical re-integration is likely to re-introduce incentives for grid owners to discriminate against competitors. General competition law can play a key role in preventing this.

The evidence, so far, of liberalising power markets does suggest that there is a real issue here. Re-integration via ownership links became an issue in the United Kingdom as soon as the initial restriction on mergers and takeovers was lifted in 1995.[27] A certain amount of vertical integration had been built into the system from the outset, since the Regional Electricity Companies (RECs) are allowed to generate 15 per cent of their power sales themselves — and are making vigorous use of this opportunity.

Table 5
Ownership of Regional Electricity Companies in England and Wales

Regional Electricity Company	Date of Initial Bid	Price (Pounds bn)	Bidder
Manweb	July 95	1.1	Scottish Power
Eastern*	July 95	2.5	Hanson
Sweb	Sept. 95	1.1	The Southern Co.
Norweb	Sept. 95	1.8	North West Water
Seeboard	Sept. 95	1.6	Central & South West
Swalec	Dec. 95	0.872	Welsh Water
Midlands	Sept. 95 May 96	1.95 1.730	Power Gen (blocked by the Government) General Public Utilities & Cinergy
Northern	Oct. 96	0.782	CalEnergy
East Midlands	Nov. 96 Jun. 98	1.3 1.9	Dominion Resources Power Gen
London	Dec. 96	1.3	Entergy
Yorkshire	Feb. 97	1.5	American Electric Power Co Inc and Power Service Co of Colorado

* Hanson subsequently demerged Eastern into part of Energy Group; in June 97, Pacificorp launched an unsuccessful 3.65 bn. Pounds bid on Energy group; in April 98, Texas Utilities made a 4.45 bn. Pounds bid for Energy group.
Source: Power United Kingdom, various issues; United Kingdom Business Park Mergers & Acquisitions, July 1998.

---

27. There is no evidence yet from other "competitive pool" markets, as their restrictions on mergers have not yet expired.

However, table 5 below shows that in three cases, generators active in the United Kingdom market, Scottish Power, PowerGen, and National Power, have issued bids to acquire, or merge with, a distributor or supplier. In two further cases, horizontal integration between electricity and water suppliers was sought.

This is by no means solely due to economies of vertical integration; the amazing profitability of the RECs, due to their greater-than-anticipated cost cutting capability, also plays a role. United Kingdom experience, however, highlights that adequate vertical separation, once introduced, is by no means guaranteed to last, and that regulators and competition authorities need to watch developments closely.

While a critical mass of market participants is necessary to support competition, competition policy must also consider the size and nature of investments in the power sector which are sunk for the most part and long term. The application of the competition law should take into account the various economies of scale and scope present in this sector.

■ Competitive Neutrality/State Aids

In many systems, entities of various legal status participate in the power sector. They may have a variety of owners — private, municipal, state and national government — and a variety of relationships to a taxpayer-financed budget and debt guarantees. They also enjoy a range of freedom from the government to make business decisions. "Competitive neutrality" means that no entity is advantaged or disadvantaged due to its ownership. A lack of neutrality can arise in a variety of ways: subsidies, transfers, special privileges such as tax exemptions and procurement set-asides and restrictions on input purchases, e.g., restrictions on choice of supplier of capital equipment or on type of labour contract. Neutrality is also undermined when a company has access to capital at lower rates because of state guarantees or where an entity receives capital infusions or loans from the state on terms and conditions not available in capital markets. In addition to these direct economic effects, neutrality is eroded when regulations or other laws, such as the competition law and private commercial law, are not applied equally regardless of ownership. In view of its importance, non-discriminatory special arrangements for the power sector have been made in some jurisdictions. For example, in Victoria, there is a legislative provision that enables the Office of the Regulator-General to appoint an administrator to a financially troubled distributor.

Security of Supply

It is important to be clear what is meant by security of supply in the power sector. Electricity is a form of final energy which uses primary energy sources as inputs and transforms them. This means that electricity has a contribution to make to overall energy security (through its potential for substitution and diversification) as well as raising the issue of security of electricity supply itself, which is essentially security of transformation. Thus, three aspects of security of supply should be distinguished:

- short-term security of transformation, *i.e.*, system reliability;
- long-term security of transformation, *i.e.*, adequate capacity investment;
- security of input energy supply, *i.e.*, fuel diversification.

■ Short-Term Security of Transformation

Short-term security of transformation, or system reliability, refers to the short-term capability of the power industry to cover demand at all times. In the past, governments have often set reliability standards for large parts of the industry and these standards were, in some cases, very stringent. They were established on the assumption that virtually all customers required the same standard of reliability.

Market liberalisation changes the perspective on these issues fundamentally. It shifts decision-making from governments to market players and it creates a "bottom-up" rather than "top-down" decision-making framework in which for the first time end users at the bottom participate in decision-making with producers. The issue is how these market players will make their decisions and how to define the remaining political responsibility to ensure that the key public policy objective of supply security is met. Specifically, the issue is of whether there is a need for governments to continue to define security of supply and set a standard or simply let markets determine this through the interplay of supply and demand.

It is now widely accepted that customer needs will vary and, in particular, that some customers can use interruptible electricity supply. Efficiency requires that suppliers offer the appropriate menu of interruptible services and related prices to all consumers who wish to have them. Such pricing arrangements have a significant potential to "shave" a system's peak, provided that interruptible consumers *do* get cut off in case of an emergency.

In the competitive part of a liberalised market there is a strong case for letting consumers determine their own contractual arrangements for electricity supply in which they will need to balance price and security considerations. They may wish to have contracts which safeguard security by specifying a "long term" price (a price that is hedged against volatility) plus a penalty payment for non-delivery. There is, however, a potential issue — not yet fully tested because liberalised markets are not yet commonplace — of whether consumers will be inclined to take the "least cost" approach and discount the importance of security and whether consumers fully appreciate the trade-off between prices and security. This may be a transitional issue but needs monitoring because of the underlying importance of ensuring effective security.

In the non-competitive part of the market among "captive" consumers, the issue is different. Governments may legitimately take the view that such consumers have to be protected from involuntary reductions in supply reliability. If price caps are part of the regulatory system, there is a particular need for caution because suppliers have an incentive to reduce service quality.

For consumers who want uninterrupted supply, this issue has been addressed in the United Kingdom and in many other countries by defining standards of service in the public electricity supply licences. An alternative would be for the regulator to fix a price per Kilowatt-hour not delivered and oblige the supplier to pay an indemnity for supply shortfalls on this basis.

Another aspect of system reliability is the provision of ancillary services needed to maintain voltage and frequency in the system, and to start the system up again in case it has broken down. These services, namely frequency and voltage support, spinning reserve and black start capability must be priced as services independent of the supply of electrical energy. These services require co-operation with the grid, whereas the same generators might compete in the supply of kilowatt-hours. The pricing of these services may need regulatory control, though no abuses have yet been detected. In practice, a conflict between competition and system reliability need not arise. Victoria in Australia is an example of power markets that have improved plant availability and reliability of supply while reducing cost.

■ Long-Term Security of Transformation

This essentially refers to the power sector's capacity for generating electricity. In the past, and in unliberalised markets, the sector tended to carry large capacity margins, some in excess of 20 per cent of peak demand. This is neither efficient, nor sustainable in a liberalised market.

Again, the issue arises whether the market can adequately provide incentives for the provision of generating capacity or whether there is a need for government intervention. The concern for the long term is that investment in generating capacity might not be sufficient to "keep the lights on", cover peak demand. The risk to which the suppliers are exposed will change since regulatory risk (whether and when costs will be passed on) will be replaced by market risk. It will not be possible any more automatically to pass on cost overruns to consumers. Utilities will also be penalised if they overestimate demand — planning, and building large-scale plant a long time ahead of need might lead to excess cost that competitors can undercut. All this suggests that electricity will become more like a "normal" market with a "normal" business cycle. The question is whether this is compatible with the requirement to cover non-interruptible demand at all times.

In principle, the price mechanism serves to fit quantity demanded to the available supply, and to give signals for investment. However, a pronounced business cycle could trigger a high degree of price volatility risk hedging via contracts for differences could conceivably become impossible. Then there would be a real question as to whether enough capacity investment would be carried out. In this situation, mothballed capacity could be drawn upon, or quick-to-build gas turbines using distillates could be constructed to fill the gaps. An extreme business cycle in the electricity market could thus exacerbate cyclicity in oil demand, which might in turn create a security problem in oil which in all likelihood would take the form of a price risk rather than a quantity risk. The longer and the more pronounced these cycles were, the more sizeable the effects on the oil market. The question here is whether investors only follow short-term price signals or whether they anticipate price trends over a longer term. Initial research shows that investment decisions are based on mid- to long-term price and demand forecasts rather than on a short-term assessment of historical price and demand developments.

■ Security of Input Fuels

The degree of diversity that naturally develops in liberalised markets remains to be seen. Suppliers to ultimate consumers, be they incumbent utilities, power marketing organisations or new generators, will be under a contractual obligation to deliver power according to their clients' risk preference (interruptible or not); non-delivery will be subject to penalty payments. Therefore, suppliers may have incentives to diversify their own supplies in order to avoid penalties. Whether there will be sufficient diversity depends partly upon the extent of short-termism which emerges in power markets and upon the cyclicity in oil demand this could cause. The issue also goes back to the likely behaviour of newly empowered consumers in liberalised markets and the premium which they are prepared to pay for security through diversity. The key development here will be the effective internalisation of all the costs of security into tariffs. Producers and suppliers will need to be motivated by customers and by the prices which customers are prepared to pay to spread their risk across fuel sources. The issue ultimately is whether diversity of primary energy is underpriced in a free market, *i.e.*, whether there remains a security externality.

If necessary, governments will need to consider action to promote particular forms of input energy, such as nuclear and renewable energy, and devise mechanisms to do this. How to provide incentives for investment in nuclear power generation is an important issue in some countries. The comments above on cross subsidies are relevant here. It is important that mechanisms be fully transparent and that they minimise distortions. Since the issue of diversity of primary energy sources arises in the entire energy market, a solution must be applied in this wider context.

Also important is the issue of "political risk", the risk of political disruption to fuel inputs to power generation. This still comes back to the underlying question of how consumers will choose to value security, and the extent to which liberalised markets will internalise effectively all the costs of security through contracts and tariffs. Risk cannot ever be removed entirely — whether in liberalised or unliberalised markets. However, the growing economic linkages between different parts of the world mean that there is a mutual interest in minimising disruptions.

The overall approach which governments should consider taking to security of supply may be as follows:

- First, the benefits of market liberalisation need to be taken into account, and it is important that the process, once engaged, should be taken as far as it can. This will avoid fractured responsibility for security of supply among governments and market players involved. Where rules remain necessary, there should be "market friendly" approaches that minimise distortion of market decisions. There is a need to give the fullest possible freedom for direct interplay between production and consumption.
- Second, governments will need to monitor the situation, for example, to track the evolution of tariffs and contracts and the investment decisions which are being taken in the new conditions.
- Third, governments need to take action if necessary to deal with market failure. This, as noted above, is already happening, for example, in relation to captive consumers and input energy diversification.

Environment

The power sector has a very significant effect on the environment. Regulatory reform and the introduction of competition raise both challenges and opportunities in this regard. It shifts decision making from government to market players and gives consumers an opportunity to make choices, rather than to have choices made on their behalf. Privatisation and corporatisation put companies at arms' length from government. Environmental regulation must be redesigned to fit this new framework, and regulation should shift toward being more transparent and incentive-based rather than a matter of direct control. Unlike security of supply, environmental objectives are very likely to require some form of regulation to make up for the market's inability to internalise effectively the environmental externalities. There is a need for specific actions to safeguard the environment, especially to restrict emissions of carbon dioxide, sulphur dioxide and nitrogen oxides.

In England and Wales, for example, electricity, coal and gas reforms led to a 25 per cent fall in the share of electricity generated from coal, from 1990/91 to 1995/96. This was due to the closure of older coal-fired plants by the incumbent non-nuclear generators and the entry of CCGT plants, which use a substantially cleaner technology. So the reform induced a shift toward gas and away from coal, as well as a shift toward younger coal plants, which resulted in a decrease in the quantity of harmful emissions from generation.[28]

Conversely, in systems which are largely based on non-fossil fuels, such as those of Norway, Sweden and Switzerland competition may well increase CO_2 emissions. Under some circumstances competition may favour a shift toward greater use of coal plants away from gas plants for base load power, or towards older, dirtier coal plants. If this is the case, there can be negative environmental effects. For example, if end-users are free to choose their suppliers, they can by-pass environmental regulations and buy from suppliers who operate with lower environmental standards, resulting in increased environmental damage. Concern about by-pass seems to be behind German utilities' complaint that their industrial electricity prices imbed higher environmental requirements than do those of other EU countries.[29] There might also be concern that "grandfathered" older plants, or dirtier plants in lower cost countries, may displace younger or domestic plants that are subject to higher environmental standards.

Most environmental effects of power sector reform are case-specific, and it is difficult to provide a general answer to these

---

28. *In this context, the United Kingdom example is often cited. What should be noted, however, is that the extent and the timing of the "dash for gas" - and the resulting environmental benefits - are a mixture of various factors, including a real cost advantage of new gas plant, reduction of coal prices through removal of market distortions in the coal market, and several structural "anomalies" in the newly-liberalised power sector, such as a failure to introduce sufficient competition in generation at the outset, a certain degree of vertical integration between generation, distribution and supply (i.e. the fact that RECs were allowed to generate 15 per cent of their power sales themselves), the fact that RECs were allowed to write long-terms CfDs for the generation subsidiaries they created, and the fact that those companies' CCGTs could bid zero into the pool and cover possible revenue shortfalls through the CfDs backed by the REC's safe customer base.*

29. *German utilities enumerate the following higher costs, relative to other European Union countries: 2 Pf for support domestic hard coal, 1.4 Pf for tighter desulfurisation requirements and 1.4 Pf for tighter requirements to bury transmission lines (Stromthemen, June 1995).*

questions. The problem is further complicated by the fact that electricity allows extraction of usable energy from otherwise unusable primary sources or larger amounts of usable energy from the same amount of primary energy via combined heat and power production, CHP, thereby helping to reduce environmental externalities. The economic viability of these technologies is also case-specific. Liberalisation, by providing non-discriminatory grid access for the first time, is likely to lead to use of these technologies where they are economic. For example, CHP capacity increased in the United Kingdom after power sector reform. In other countries, where CHP has been developed due to government support programmes, CHP capacity will no longer expand.

■ Taxes and Fees

One way to internalise the environmental costs of emissions is through taxes and fees. A carbon tax is already used in Denmark, Sweden, Norway, Finland and the Netherlands. There are also energy taxes or fees on sulphur and nitrogen emissions in various countries. A liberalised energy market with more independent actors and less direct government involvement needs a framework of regulations or economic instruments within which market forces can operate freely. The implementation of such economic instruments is facilitated by international or regional co-operation and harmonisation. In the short run, this may be difficult to achieve, and it may be that special transitional arrangements are needed so that individual countries are not forced to abandon environmental economic instruments because of competition from countries with lower, and less costly, levels of environmental protection.

■ Energy Subsidies

Energy subsidies have historically played a crucial role and need to be addressed in any regulatory reform programme which seeks to meet environmental objectives. The reform of energy subsidies can have environmental as well as direct economic benefits. Studies by the World Bank and OECD (Larsen and Shah 1992; Burniaux et al., 1992) found energy subsidies of over $ 200 billion worldwide, mostly in developing countries and the countries of the former Soviet Union. They found that eliminating those subsidies would lead to reduction in carbon dioxide emissions of well over one billion tonnes by 2010.

In 1994-96, the OECD carried out a study ("Reforming Energy and Transport Subsidies", OECD 1997) on the environmental effects of removing energy subsidies in its Member countries; in some of the case studies, the geographical scope was wider. Key findings from the study are:

- Carbon dioxide reductions achieved by removing selected subsidies can, indeed, be substantial although probably not so large as suggested by some economic models.

- The types of subsidies whose removal would lead to the greatest environmental benefit are grants and other forms of budgetary and price support for coal production, especially where these supports are combined with supports for electricity industry investment.

- Subsidies and tax exemptions are provided for residential and large industrial consumers of electricity in many countries; in some countries, they are very significant. Removing these supports would lead to reduced electricity consumption, and reduced the environmental impacts of such consumption.

- Removing some subsidies would have negative environmental effects. For example, subsidies are used in many countries to support renewable energy[30] and energy conservation.

---

30. Unlike hydro-power, whose economically recoverable, and environmentally acceptable, potential is nearly exhausted in most OECD countries, non-hydro renewables have hardly any measurable impact on environmental emissions at present: they contribute less than one per cent of IEA countries' total electricity generation. This ratio is only exceeded at country level in some cases such as New Zealand, where geothermal (which itself is burdened with environmental emissions, i.e. acidic effluents) has a share of around 10 per cent of generation. That non-hydro renewables can make a measurable contribution towards alleviating environmental problems holds only for the future, and under the assumption that their prices come down significantly, or that governments create regulatory frameworks or support measures that create a supply push or demand pull which leads to much accelerated market uptake of renewables. Failing this, the negative impact of subsidy removal for renewables merely exists as a remote possibility. At present and, according to current trends, in the foreseeable future, the contribution of renewables is too insignificant to have any noticeable influence on emissions levels. There are many reasons why societies and the governments that represent them may want to keep renewables research going and subsidise a certain amount of renewables into the market. One example is the contingency value of renewables i.e. having some non-fossil technology ready and tested to prepare for possible climate change.

- Most energy-related subsidies are provided for social reasons, to reduce energy costs for low income households and to protect employment in coal mining and energy intensive industries. Any process of subsidy reform would need to include consideration of the original rationale for the subsidy, and it might be important to introduce compensatory measures to avoid negative social effects.

Tradable Emissions Permits

Subsidies are not, in theory, the most market-friendly approach to environmental regulation. One alternative approach which actually uses the market (rather than working against it) is tradable emissions permits. Under such a system, governments or regulators specify a total maximum quantity of emissions of perhaps specify local maximums, issue the corresponding permits for emissions, require utilities to install sensors on smokestacks, and allow such permits to be traded among permit holders. This type of control is compatible with a competitive market for generation. It works best for environmental problems that have relatively few sources, which makes the power sector an ideal area for its application.

In the United States, 1990 amendments to the Clean Air Act moved the control of sulphur dioxide emissions toward a market mechanism in two ways. First, they allowed power plants to comply with sulphur dioxide emission performance standards rather than to strict emissions controls requiring the use of specified technology: this allowed competition among compliance technologies, thereby reducing the cost of attaining any given level of compliance. Second, they allowed some trading of sulphur dioxide emissions permits among firms. A regional programme in southern California, in which emission permits for nitrogen oxides can be traded, was implemented in 1994. Unlike the national programme for sulphur dioxide, the southern California programme has restrictions on the location of traded emissions to help prevent "hot spots", that is, regions of very high pollutant concentration.

In both of these programmes, regulators can improve the environment, reduce the costs of achieving a given level of environmental quality, and provide flexibility for economic growth (Economic Report of the President, 1996, pp. 148-9). Indeed, one estimate of the annual cost savings from the sulphur dioxide emissions allowances programme, as compared with a command and control system for the same level of emissions, is up to $1.7 billion after 2000.[31] Another estimate that takes into account the restrictions placed on utilities from participating fully in the program is a cost saving of $4.19 billion over the period 1995-2005 (Winebrake, Bernstein and Farrell 1995). One estimate of the cost savings from the United States' nation-wide acid rain emissions trading programme is 20 to 50 per cent by 2010.

In addition to these effects, the effectiveness of scrubbers has improved and their costs decreased by more than 40 per cent (IEA 1995). Further, because emissions trading creates efficiencies to which no one has "prior claim", it is possible for industry and environmentalists to agree on tougher (i.e., cleaner) standards where there is trading than if there were a command-and-control system (Loeb 1995).

Such programmes require that the regulator have a certain amount of information, including that necessary to set the number of permits (totals and, if necessary, sub-totals for particularly environmentally-sensitive regions). Information is also necessary to provide incentives for utilities to switch to new systems of environmental control which lower the cost of meeting specified environmental goals. When the individual cost of reducing emissions is not known to the regulator, this can imply a departure from the optimum when the cost is known where the amount of reduction in emissions is set so that the social cost of emissions equals the social benefit of such reduction (Lewis 1996). Finally, the

---

31. The estimate is from the Electric Power Research Institute, *Integrated Analysis of Fuel, Technology and Emission Allowance Markets: Electric Utility Responses to the Clean Air Act Amendments of 1990* (EPRI TR 102510, November 1993). Assumptions include that there would be mainly intra-industry trade. Inter-industry trade could result in additional annual savings of US$600 million to 1.2 billion (Rose, 1995).

cost of gathering and using the information, as well as other administrative costs, would enter into the decision whether to switch to the new regime. Overall, however, this approach has been positive and could be promising.

■ Energy Efficiency

A third mechanism for meeting environmental objectives is the use of energy efficiency programmes which help to reduce emissions. Many utilities have energy efficiency programmes which aim either to reduce total energy use or to shift peak usage to off-peak periods.[32] Usage shifting may or may not have an environmental effect, depending on the technology used along the load curve. Some programmes are of command-and-control type, prescribing home, office and factory energy efficiency investments. Participating end-users receive incentive payments from the utility. These incentive payments, utility-related programme costs and "lost revenue" recovery (because of the smaller quantity of energy sold) are gathered from all customers in the service area. Such cross-subsidies are inconsistent with liberalised markets and would therefore require some redesign in order to assign costs appropriately. End users should make the decision about whether and how best to conserve energy in the face of prices that better reflect the real cost of electric power. Provided the cost of metering and information management drops sufficiently low, some of the new programmes could involve consumers taking an active role in their own load management, such as reducing total usage or shifting some use to off-peak periods (Houston 1994 and Joskow 1994). These programmes would actually mimic peak load pricing.

There is no *a priori* general direction for the environmental effects from economic regulatory reform; the effect of the regulatory change varies from circumstance to circumstance. However, the

---

32. It should be noted that "peak shaving" efficiency programmes have had more of a noticeable effect in the aggregate than "energy reducing" ones: the latter have not managed to dent, let alone curb, electricity demand growth in OECD countries, while the former can have a small but noticeable impact on individual utilities' load curves.

reform of economic regulation creates an opportunity also to reform environmental regulation towards more market-based approaches, so that given levels of emissions abatement can be attained at lower cost and subsidies can be better directed toward the intended recipients. Some of these market-based approaches, such as taxes and emissions permit trading, have already been implemented. However, as with all reforms from a command and control system, incentive-compatible programmes must take account of both the *status quo* and the information available to various parties.

Other Policy Objectives

Social and customer protection objectives are also very important. A key objective is consumer protection. During discussions of regulatory reform, concern is often expressed that consumers may suffer negative consequences. These concerns are important in view of the role electric power plays in modern society.

One major concern is that consumers may suffer a degradation in quality of service. In some reforms, consumers have been given explicit new rights. In the United Kingdom, consumers enjoy guaranteed standards of performance, such as restoration of service after an outage and adequate notice of planned interruptions of supply. They have the right to more frequent meter reading, and there are new codes of practice for dealing with consumer complaints. Consumers have the right to complain to an independent regulator. In Victoria, the Office of the Regulator-General sets standards through the licensing process and can financially penalise licensees who do not meet the standards. The office also provides a fact sheet, available to consumers, advising them of their rights.

In Finland, during the drafting of the Electricity Market Act, the Consumer Ombudsman stressed the need to include an obligation for retailers to supply those of their customers who are outside the competitive market and to forbid the cutting off of electricity to consumers whose home heating depended on it. Another area of concern was to ensure that breaches of the contract, such as interruptions of supply, were appropriately dealt with under the new law. In the event, the law was passed with the statement that it should be complemented with additional consumer protection clauses.

Provision of universal service is important to protect the poorest members of society. This has two dimensions: the obligation to supply, and disconnection policy. In many power markets with competitive elements, the abolition of the utility's exclusive right to supply has required a re-definition of the obligation to supply that was often combined with it. In many cases, this was accomplished by obliging grid owners to connect any consumer who expressed a wish to be connected. In some cases, such as the United Kingdom or Victoria, the supply licences specify a supplier of last resort. In OECD countries, unlike in many developing countries, the fraction of the population which is too poor to pay for electricity is small, since for most consumers, including industrial consumers, electricity constitutes less than 5 per cent of their budget. Consumer disconnection is therefore not a wide-spread phenomenon. Moreover, consumers now have more current information about their charges for electric power. This enables them to take more control over their usage decisions. For example, pre-payment meters or smart-card meters in the home let consumers know instantly their costs for electric power. Subsidies of electric power usage could be targeted to low-income persons through the form of smart-cards issued through social services providers (O'Connor *et al.*).

The lower prices expected from power sector reform may provide part of the solution in themselves. In addition, standards for disconnection policy are often defined more clearly in licences in competitive power markets. In the United Kingdom, for example, this has led to a sharp reduction of residential consumers disconnections for debt: between 1991/92 and 1995/96, the figure has fallen from a total of 41,018 disconnections to just 674 in England and Wales (OFFER: Report on Customer Services 1995/96).

Education plays an important role in giving consumers enough information to take advantage of their new options. The transition from having only one possible provider with a very limited menu of offerings, to general menus offered by several providers has already been experienced, in some countries, by consumers of telecommunications. In principle, one would expect similar issues of consumer learning to arise, along with the additional uncertainty associated with electric power (unusual weather, unexpected changes in fuel costs). As noted in the section on financial markets, there are financial instruments by which consumers can shed this risk in the same way as they already reduce risk through insurance contracts.

REGULATORY REFORM: TRANSITION ISSUES

Regulatory reform is bound to raise transition issues. This is not peculiar to the power sector. One question is whether the long term benefits of regulatory reform will outweigh the transitional costs. The answer depends to some degree on the performance of the sector prior to reform and liberalisation. The question may also need to be asked, however, whether a good pre-reform performance can be sustained. Reform in one country is likely to have some important effects onto non-reforming countries (e.g., technological advances and power trade across international borders). If regulatory reform does in fact provide large benefits, the standards by which non-reforming sectors are judged may be raised. If others are reforming their markets, it may be difficult to maintain the status quo.

The performance of the Victoria power industry prior to liberalisation, for example, was assessed as abysmal by industry observers. Even though the pain of uprooting the industry and getting it off to a fresh start was dramatic, it was clear from the outset that the potential efficiency gains were enormous and more than justified the action taken. In markets which function better at the outset the efficiency gains may be smaller, but so will be the cost of making the transition.

Stranded Costs

A key transition issue is stranded costs. Both in countries where electric utilities are privately owned and were previously subject to a rate-of-return form of economic regulation and in countries where the assets are owned by various levels of government, an important policy issue is the treatment of stranded costs. Stranded costs are the unamortised costs of prior investments that are scheduled for recovery through regulated monopoly rates but would not be recovered under competition. Stranded costs are specific to the transition between regulatory regimes. Under former regulatory regimes there was a "regulatory compact" under which companies undertook large, sunk investments with the understanding that regulators would ensure that their rate of return on capital would be just and reasonable. With a change in regulatory philosophy the recovery of stranded costs is a matter of justice as well as of economic efficiency. Sunk investments — such as many of the assets in the power sector — will be made in the future only if a government can credibly assure the potential investor that the rules will not change in a way that harms him (Economic Report of the President, pp. 186-8).

Stranded costs may arise when assets are under private ownership, as well as government ownership. For example, a municipally-owned utility may have made an approved sunk investment that would have been recovered under the former system of regulation but which will not be recovered under the new system of regulation.

Stranded costs can be large: it was estimated at up to $135 billion for the next ten years for privately-owned United States utilities according to a report by Moody's Investors Service.[33] Losses on stranded cost were estimated to amount to 80 per cent of private utilities' total equity or 1/4 of the industry's total assets between 1996 and 2005. Utilities in the high-price North-East and West are worst off, together accounting for 40 per cent of the total damage. According to the report, at least 10 nuclear plants, amounting to 10 per cent of total United States operating nuclear plant, may be closed due to deregulation. More may be mothballed. Other estimates range from approximately half to more than twice this figure.

Once the decision is taken to allow utilities to recover stranded costs (at least partly), the first difficulty regulators face is to determine how much of the assets really are stranded, since the

---

33. Moody's Investors Service: *Stranded Costs Will Threaten Credit Quality of United States Electrics*, 1995.

utilities cannot be relied upon to produce unbiased information on this issue. One way of solving this dilemma may be to auction off the assets and thus let the market determine their worth. Other regulatory reforms suggest that a significant portion of stranded costs can be avoided through the utilisation of new technologies and development of creative ideas for alternative uses.

Next, a mechanism has to be found to allocate the extra cost. This decision can affect the efficiency of markets; if a stranded cost "fee" introduces a wedge between price and marginal cost, then inefficiently small quantities of electric power will be purchased. If a stranded cost "fee" applies to only a subset of end-users, then it may be perceived as unfair (Economic Report of the President, p. 188). In California, the decision was made to collect a fee charged on the wires, *i.e.* allocated among customers as costs are currently allocated among them, but for the charge to end in 2005.[34] However, it has been proposed by the regulator that the utilities earn a lower although still fair rate of return on their investment-related transition costs, on the grounds that these are lower risk investments.

Social Costs

Stranded costs are not the only type of transition cost. It has become clear that electricity market reform, and especially the introduction of competition, is a powerful mechanism to improve micro-economic efficiency, but it can also produce macro-economic problems such as abandonment of unprofitable power plants, or primary fuel extraction operations, leading to unemployment and social hardship. At macro level, these effects are only temporary: a separate study by the OECD shows that labour released from companies which have become uneconomic due to competition is absorbed back into the economy quickly

---

34. *However, it has been proposed by the regulator that the utilities earn a lower - although still "fair" - rate of return on their investment-related transition costs, asserting that these are lower risk investments.*

enough not to create major problems. But the labour released and the labour absorbed will in all likelihood not be the same people, because it may be difficult to find or to train for other jobs. Job shedding in the electricity supply industry has been very large: in the United Kingdom, for example, National Power and PowerGen reduced the number of their direct employees by 65 per cent and 53 per cent, respectively, between 1991 and 1995. Electricity sector reform creates winners and losers. Any regulatory reform does this, but the extent of the pain may be greater in the power sector than in some others, because it has been so protected for such a long time.

The economies of Central and Eastern Europe may provide a useful lesson. Poland chose a radical, high speed reform path, and saw its GDP plummet more quickly and, at first, more deeply than those of its neighbours. However, the quick and intense pain of transition was followed by an earlier, and more vigorous, improvement in macro-economic performance indicators. One conclusion that may be drawn for electricity market reform is: think hard, but move quickly and vigorously.

Sequencing of Reforms

The sequence in which reform takes place is also crucial for its success. If one begins with state-owned assets, the legal and regulatory apparatus should first be put in place, then major restructuring should be accomplished, then privatisation can occur (Besant-Jones, p. 27). An advantage of having some time before the privatisation is to permit the regulator and potential investors to learn and adjust.

Evolution of Regulatory Reform

The reform of the power sector is an evolutionary process — a number of unresolved questions remain, and the future development of reform will depend on the experience gathered. It is important to set up a robust reform process so that learning and adjustments will take place and changes will be made in a transparent way acceptable to power sector companies, users, regulators and voters. One can indeed view the reform of the power sector as a co-evolution of the industry, its markets and its regulators.

An evolutionary approach is also important for another reason. As markets evolve and become more efficient, some regulation may no longer be necessary since the public policy objectives which generate regulation may be met by the market itself. This may, for example, be the case for social objectives, where suppliers may find it is in their own economic interest to improve services.

REGULATORY REFORM: WHAT DOES IT DELIVER?

This section considers not only what has been achieved but also what may be expected. Given that no competitive power market has operated for more than five years, none has yet completed the stage of transition. Therefore, the results presented here do not provide conclusive evidence of the long term benefits — or disadvantages — of power sector reform. The cost and price reductions quoted below are due to several linked factors, including liberalisation, technological advances (CCGTs) and lowered input prices (gas, but also coal). Moreover, since the assets in the power sector tend to be long-lived and, to a large degree, sunk, results must be expected to emerge relatively slowly.

Industry Performance

The first expected benefit from market liberalisation is improved industrial performance through a reduction in the cost of supplying electricity. This may be achieved through:

- higher capital productivity resulting from greater plant availability, improved efficiency in the operation of existing generating facilities, reduced excess capacity, improved investment and technology choices;

- higher labour productivity resulting from reduced overstaffing, sick leave, absenteeism, etc.

There is some evidence of this happening. In the United Kingdom, power generators have made substantial increases in productivity. Labour productivity, approximated as kWh generated per employee, doubled in National Power and PowerGen after privatisation. Nuclear Electric was not privatised until 31 March 1996 when it became, together with Scottish Nuclear, but excluding its old Magnox plants, British Energy. Nuclear Electric's output per employee rose by 60 per cent between 1991-92 and 1994-95. The availability of its plants greatly increased. Taken together, these improvements led to a decline in nuclear generating cost in excess of 40 per cent between 1990 and 1995.

In New Zealand, there is evidence of cost savings through internal efficiency gains in generation and transmission of the order of 10-15 per cent (about 3 per cent of total wholesale electricity prices) excluding finance, tax and fuel (Culy, Read and Wright, pp. 3 and 8).

The introduction of competition in Victoria has improved labour and capital productivity indices considerably. The industry employed a total of 24 000 staff in 1989; this figure has fallen to 6 500 today. The coal-fired base load plants Yallourn W and Hazelwood, which reported 60 per cent annual availability in 1991/92, and a 30-year average of 62 per cent availability (Hazelwood), were available at 87 per cent and 80 per cent in 1995/96.[35] Overall, plant availability increased by the equivalent to 700 MW of additional capacity, slightly more than 10 per cent of installed capacity. Simultaneously, supply reliability increased: outage minutes per year and per customer were reduced from an average of 510 in 1989/90 to 266 in 1993/94, and 260 in 1994/95. The distribution companies have also improved productivity: the smallest increased the number of customers per employee from 390 to 510 from October 1994 to January 1996. The average contract wholesale cost of energy was AS$0.04/kWh in 1994/95, 20 per cent lower than in the previous year.

Industry performance may also be considered in terms of new market entry, a powerful stimulus to cost reductions by incumbents and lower prices to consumers. In New Zealand there has been significant new entry of about 760 MW (note that this phenomenon was regulated into existence by disallowing any capacity expansion by the incumbent Electricity Corporation of New Zealand).

---

35. Source: Victorian Power Exchange (VPX).

One of the main shortcomings of United Kingdom liberalisation is the insufficient horizontal disaggregation of the generation business due to the fact that the former CEGB was split into only three separate companies. Two of the three generating companies, National Power and PowerGen, held 80 per cent of the generating market, and owned the marginal plant that set the Pool price an even greater percentage of the time. Since then, there has been new entry into generation, and the shares of the two large companies have fallen, but the regulator, giving evidence before the House of Commons in 1996, when their shares totalled 45 per cent, said that he was "not satisfied with the present extent of competitiveness either in the pool or in generation". In early 1997, electricity sales generated by new entrants are still only 10 per cent of the total.

Consumer Benefits

One of the main benefits of market liberalisation occurs when reduced supply costs of electricity are translated into lower prices for consumers. The expectation is that lower prices will be achieved through competitive pressure to reduce costs and prices to marginal cost. Here there is much positive evidence. The picture, however, may vary according to the category of consumer — industrial, commercial, retail.

In the United Kingdom, average real electricity prices had fallen by 13 per cent by the beginning of 1997, compared with 1990. Over the same period, the average real price paid by small industrial and service consumers declined by 19 per cent.[36]

In New Zealand since 1985, commercial and smaller industrial consumers have experienced lower prices, but average domestic prices in real terms are virtually the same in 1995 as in 1985, although they were lower in 1991. Average commercial electricity prices felt by about 25 per cent from 1985 to 1995.

---

34. *Oral communications by the United Kingdom regulator, Professor Stephen K. Littlechild, at the Second World Conference on Restructuring and Regulation of the Electricity Market in Vasteras, Sweden: 3-4 February 1997.*

In Norway, most prices had fallen by 1994, with price decreases for commercial customers larger than those for residential customers. Wholesale prices had declined substantially. In 1995, both wholesale and retail prices had increased relative to 1994. These price changes may reflect changes in weather rather than the effects of the reform, however.

As well as lower prices, reform can be expected to bring better customer service through the availability of a menu of more efficient pricing structures, especially time-of-day pricing and interruptible service pricing. Energy consulting services may also emerge as the market gears up to meet a range of actual and potential customer needs. Innovation of various kinds is stimulated by competition.

An issue which does concern many governments embarking on reform is whether quality of service will suffer, especially for vulnerable consumer groups. Many governments are choosing to set rules and standards in the early days of market liberalisation, in order to ensure that consumers are not disadvantaged. Price controls are the most obvious example. The expectation is that as competition takes hold, these arrangements may be dismantled. Time will tell.

CONCLUSIONS AND RECOMMENDATIONS

Conclusions

Regulatory reform and liberalisation of the power sector present significant opportunities as well as some challenges. The strong expectation is that they will yield important short and long term benefits in terms of improving economic efficiency, lowering costs and consumer prices and stimulating economic growth and competitiveness. These benefits have started to show clearly in those countries which have already liberalised. In some former state-owned companies, labour productivity has improved by as much as 60 per cent and generating costs have declined by as much as 40 per cent. In other countries, annual availability of generating plants has improved significantly (from 60 per cent to 87 per cent), customer outages have been reduced, distribution company productivity has improved, and prices have been reduced by 20 per cent in wholesale markets and from 13 to 19 per cent in retail markets. Other significant long term gains are expected, notably further efficiency, technical gains and service innovations, including a wider variety of pricing structures and contracts. There are wider economic benefits from improved economic efficiency in the sector, given that electricity is an input to almost all goods and services.

Regulatory reform affects a wide number of policy objectives such as the environment and security of supply, not just the objective of increased economic efficiency. By triggering far-reaching changes in economic structure, control and output, it raises issues of how best to meet these objectives in new conditions. However, there is no evidence at this stage that these other objectives will be adversely affected, provided that care is taken to update the regulatory framework. In the case of the environment, a framework including greenhouse gas emissions trading is likely to be more effective than current policies. In the case of security of supply, market decisions may be expected to reflect adequately the short term cost of security. However, the impact of market liberalisation on investments in long term generating capacity and diversity of fuel inputs to power generators is not yet fully clear.

The introduction of competition into the power sector can take a number of forms. The current natural monopoly in the operation of transmission and the physical behaviour of electricity have implications for the level of competition that can be introduced. Much depends on the starting point, including energy situation and trading options, in a particular country, but it is important to keep in mind the common goals and elements of these restructuring efforts.

Reform and market liberalisation is an ongoing process and it is in its early days. There is a long period of transition from regulated monopolies to properly functioning markets. It is important to be aware of the various elements of a transition regime and to frame good policies for this. These elements include the role of general competition law, the issue of stranded costs and pricing issues, among others. The basic framework for regulatory reform must meet the needs of transition, establishing non-discriminatory and transparent adjustment mechanisms, as well as having the capacity to adapt and evolve to deal with the longer term, when market liberalisation has settled down.

Recommendations

- Governments should expand the scope for competition in the power sector. In doing so, they need to clarify their key policy objectives for the sector, such as improved efficiency, as well as the important linkages with other public policies such as security of supply and environmental protection.

- The key elements in the reform process which need early definition are the power sector's ownership, its structure and the regulatory structure. Adequate competition will only be established if these three elements are adequately tackled. In addition, the overall regulatory framework needs to be non-discriminatory and transparent, and provide sufficient information to market participants.

- As regards ownership, corporatisation with incentives will improve efficiency. But, in the long run, privatisation is best.

- As regards structure, two basic models of competition have evolved so far, the competitive pool model and the grid access model, and these can take a number of forms. There are many common elements between these two models; both involve at least:
  - a certain degree of vertical separation between monopoly activities (transmission and distribution) and potentially competitive activities (generation and supply),
  - circumscribed grid access rules that ensure open and fair access, and
  - adequate competition in the competitive activities from the outset.

The vertical separation aims to eliminate discrimination against competitors by vertically integrated companies. Both models look promising although there is more experience with the pool model. Whichever model is selected, it is essential that the elements of the market which are opened to competition be allowed to function and interact as liberalised markets, not subject to interference.

In the competitive pool model, the three main requirements listed above are necessary, as well as the establishment of a competitive pool for dispatch decision making. In this model, the vertical separation is either corporate or functional.

In the grid access model, the three main requirements listed in the fourth recommendation are necessary. This model typically involves accounting separation rather than stronger forms of vertical separation. Where accounting separation is chosen, the regulatory system must ensure that firms in the competitive part of the market have non-discriminatory access to monopoly facilities and must prevent anti-competitive cross subsidies. If accounting separation proves inadequate in practice, corporate or functional separation should be considered.

- As regards regulatory structure, independence of the regulator from commercial and day-to-day political pressures is essential.

- The terms of access to the transmission grid, which for the present remains a natural monopoly, need regulation, which should cover pricing. Despite its complexity, nodal pricing is likely to form part of any efficient transmission pricing scheme.

- Governments should consider whether price controls to end-users are necessary. They may be necessary in the transition to competitive markets and for captive consumers. Price controls should seek to maximise industry efficiency, as well as protect consumers. Governments should consider how long price controls are necessary before the market can safely be left to take over.

- Governments need to exercise particular care with subsidies and cross subsidies, as they distort economically efficient behaviour and pricing. Direct and open subsidies are preferable to hidden cross subsidies. Subsidies should be transparently linked to clear policy objectives. They should be kept under review, as the need for that may disappear as markets take over.

- The general competition law should be applied to the power sector except for those aspects which are covered by rules specific to it. Governments need to be particularly vigilant about the application of general competition law in the transition to liberalised markets. In the absence of sector-specific rules, governments should consider whether their general competition law and enforcement mechanisms are adequate to deal with the power sector and its complexities, and strengthen them if necessary.

- Governments should monitor the issue of security of supply in liberalising power markets. Within the new framework of reform and the introduction of competition, they should seek to create the right climate for long term investment which adequately responds to the issue of diversity of supply in the entire energy market. A regulatory framework which emphasises transparency, non-discrimination and stability will help this objective. Since the issue of diversity of primary energy sources arises in the entire energy market, a solution must be applied in this wider context.

- Governments must adapt environmental regulation and policy instruments to the altered industry structure, including exploiting the opportunities afforded by market liberalisation for better market-based approaches to environmental regulation, such as tradable emissions permits.

- Stranded costs (unamortised costs of investments carried out under a previous regulatory regime which would not be recovered in the new competitive market conditions) need to be addressed. Governments must ensure that the incentives for future investment in the sector are not damaged and minimise the extent of costs that are recovered in the transition period by providing strong incentives to mitigate stranded costs.

- Governments should review critically, and at regular intervals, whether regulation is still needed to meet their underlying objectives, as liberalised markets get into their stride. Where the need for regulation remains, the mechanisms chosen should be market compatible.

BIBLIOGRAPHY

ARMSTRONG, Mark; COWAN, Simon and VICKERS, John, 1994. *Regulatory Reform: Economic Analysis and the British Experience*, MIT Press: London.

ATKINSON, S.E. and HALVORSEN R., 1986."The relative efficiency of public and private firms in a regulated environment: The case of U.S. electric utilities", *Journal of Public Economics*, Vol. 29, pp. 281-284.

Australian Competition & Consumer Commission, ACCC Network Pricing Forum, unpublished.

BESANT-JONES, John E., 1996. "The England and Wales Electricity Model — Option or Warning for Developing Countries", *Private Sector*, The World Bank Group, March, pp. 25-28.

BITRAN, Eduardo and SERRA, Pablo, 1995. "Regulation of Privatised Utilities: lessons from the Chilean experience", mimeo, 4 October.

BLUMSTEIN, Carl and BUSHNELL, Jim, 1994. "A Guide to the Blue Book: Issues in California's Electric Industry Restructuring and Reform", *The Electricity Journal*, September, pp. 18-29.

CAVE, Martin and DOYLE, Chris, 1994. "Access pricing in network utilities in theory and practice", *Utilities Policy*, July, pp. 181-189.

Council of Economic Advisers (United States), 1996. *Economic Report of the President*.

CRUZ, Juan Manuel, 1996. "Regulatory Management in an Open Market Economy: Notes on Deregulation and Promotion of Competition", mimeo, 17 August.

CULY, J.G.; READ, E.G. and WRIGHT, B.D., 1996. "The Evolution of New Zealand's Electricity Supply Industry", *International Comparisons of Electricity Regulation*, Richard J. Gilbert and Edward P. Kahn, eds., Cambridge University Press.

GILBERT, Richard J.; KAHN, Edward P. and NEWBERY, David M., 1996."Introduction: International comparisons in electricity regulation",

International Comparisons of Electricity Regulation, Richard J. Gilbert and Edward P. Kahn, eds., Cambridge University Press.

GRAY, Philip (editor), 1996. "Industry Structure and Regulation in Infrastructure: a Cross-Country Survey", *PSD Occasional Paper No. 25*, Private Sector Development Department, The World Bank.

HJALMARSSON, Lennart, 1996. "From Club-regulation to Market Competition in the Scandinavian Electricity Supply Industry", *International Comparisons of Electricity Regulation*, Richard J. Gilbert and Edward P. Kahn, eds., Cambridge University Press.

HOGAN, W.W., 1994. "An efficient bilateral market needs a pool". Presentation given at California Public Utilities Commission Hearing, San Francisco, 4 August.

HOUSTON, Douglas A., 1994. "Can Energy Markets Drive DSM?" *Electricity Journal*, November, pp. 46-55.

JOSKOW, Paul L., 1994. "More from the Guru of Energy Efficiency: `There Must be a Pony!" *Electricity Journal*, May, pp. 50-61.

JOSKOW, Paul L. and SCHMALENSEE, Richard, 1983. *Markets for Power*, MIT Press.

KWACZEK, Adrienne S. and KERR William A., 1989. "Canadian Exports of Electricity to the U.S.: International Competitiveness or International Risk Bearing?", *World Competition*.

LALOR, R. Peter and GARCIA, Hernan, 1996. "Reshaping Power Markets — Lessons from Chile and Argentina", *Private Sector*, The World Bank Group, March, pp. 29-32.

LEWIS, Tracey R., 1996. "Protecting the Environment when Costs and Benefits are Privately Known", *Rand Journal of Economics*, vol. 27, no. 4, winter, pp. 819-847.

LITTLECHILD, Stephen, 1995. "Competition in Electricity: Retrospective and Prospect", *Utility Regulation: Challenge and Response* ed. by M.E. Beesley, Institute of Economic Affairs.

LOEB, Alan P., 1995. "Addressing the Public's Goals for Environmental Regulation When Communicating Acid Rain Allowance Trades", *Electricity Journal*, May, pp. 55-63.

MOEN, Jan and HAMRIN, Jan, 1996. "Regulation and Competition Without Privatization: Norway's Experience", *Electricity Journal*, March, pp. 37-44.

Monopolies and Mergers Commission, 1996. *PowerGen plc and Midlands Electricity plc: A Report of the Proposed Merger*, London: HMSO.

Monopolies and Mergers Commission, 1996. *National Power plc and Southern Electric plc: A Report of the Proposed Merger*, London: HMSO.

NEWBERY, David M., 1995. "Regulatory Policies and Reform in the Electricity Supply Industry", *Regulatory Policies and Reform: A Comparative Perspective*, ed. by Claudio R. Frischtak, World Bank.

Norwegian Competition Authority, 1996. *The Reform of the Norwegian Electricity Sector*.

O'CONNOR, Philip R.; JACOBSON, Erik B. and BARNICH, Terrence L., 1995. "Regulation or Technology? Low-income Electric Customers and the Transition to Competition", *Public Utilities Fortnightly*, 15 November.

OECD, 1994. *Electricity Supply Industry*.

OECD, 1995. Proceeding of the OECD/World Bank Conference on Competition and Regulation in Network Infrastructure Industries, 28 June - 1 July 1994, OCDE/GD(95)87.

OKURE, Tom U.U., 1995. "Competitive Pricing of Energy Services in New York State: Current Trends and Issues", *Electricity Journal*, January/February.

OREN, Shmuel S.; SPILLER, Pablo T.; VARAIYA, Pravin and WU, Felix, 1995. "Nodal Prices and Transmission Rights: A Critical Appraisal", *The Electricity Journal*, April, pp. 24-35.

POLLITT, M.G., 1994. "Technical Efficiency in Electric Power Plants". Mimeo, Faculty of Economics, Cambridge, UK. Cambridge University.

ROSE, Kenneth, 1995. "Twelve Common Myths of Allowance Trading: Improving the Level of Discussion", *Electricity Journal*, May, pp. 64-69.

SO, Jae and SHIN, Ben, 1996. "The Private Infrastructure Industry — Company Approaches", *Private Sector*, special edition on Infrastructure, June, pp. 9-12.

SPILLER, Pablo T. and MARTORELL, Luis Viana, 1996. "How should it be done? Electricity regulation in Argentina, Brazil, Uruguay, and Chile", *International Comparisons of Electricity Regulation*, Richard J. Gilbert and Edward P. Kahn, eds., Cambridge University Press.

STAHLKOPF, K., 1996. "The Second Silicon Revolution", *Electricity Transmission Pricing and Technology*, Einhorn, M. and Siddiqi, R., Boston, Dordrecht and Londonough.

STALON, Charles G., 1995. "Governance Problems in the U.S. Electric Industry that Complicate Restructuring", Mimeo presented at International Seminar on Comparative Experiences of Regulation of the Electric Power Sector, Buenos Aires, 10 November.

Treasury Corporation of Victoria, 1996. *Victorian Economic Review*, March-June.

TROUGHTON, Peter, 1996. "Reforming the Victorian Electricity Supply Industry", Mimeo, January.

Wall Street Journal, 1996. "German Manufacturers Force Power Monopoly To Reduce High Rates", by Matt Marshall, 12/13 July, p. 1.

WINEBRAKE, James; BERNSTEIN, Mark A. and FARRELL, Alex, 1995. "Estimating the Impacts of Restrictions on Utility Participation in the SO2 Allowance Market", *Electricity Journal*, May, pp. 50-54.

World Bank, 1995. *Bureaucrats in Business: The Economics and Politics of Government Ownership*, Oxford University Press: New York.

MAIN SALES OUTLETS OF OECD PUBLICATIONS
PRINCIPAUX POINTS DE VENTE DES PUBLICATIONS DE L'OCDE

AUSTRALIA – AUSTRALIE
D.A. Information Services
648 Whitehorse Road, P.O.B 163
Mitcham, Victoria 3132 Tel. (03) 9210.7777
 Fax: (03) 9210.7788

AUSTRIA – AUTRICHE
Gerold & Co.
Graben 31
Wien I Tel. (0222) 533.50.14
 Fax: (0222) 512.47.31.29

BELGIUM – BELGIQUE
Jean De Lannoy
Avenue du Roi, Koningslaan 202
B-1060 Bruxelles Tel. (02) 538.51.69/538.08.41
 Fax: (02) 538.08.41

CANADA
Renouf Publishing Company Ltd.
5369 Canotek Road
Unit 1
Ottawa, Ont. K1J 9J3 Tel. (613) 745.2665
 Fax: (613) 745.7660
Stores:
71 1/2 Sparks Street
Ottawa, Ont. K1P 5R1 Tel. (613) 238.8985
 Fax: (613) 238.6041
12 Adelaide Street West
Toronto, QN M5H 1L6 Tel. (416) 363.3171
 Fax: (416) 363.5963
Les Éditions La Liberté Inc.
3020 Chemin Sainte-Foy
Sainte-Foy, PQ G1X 3V6 Tel. (418) 658.3763
 Fax: (418) 658.3763

Federal Publications Inc.
165 University Avenue, Suite 701
Toronto, ON M5H 3B8 Tel. (416) 860.1611
 Fax: (416) 860.1608
Les Publications Fédérales
1185 Université
Montréal, QC H3B 3A7 Tel. (514) 954.1633
 Fax: (514) 954.1635

CHINA – CHINE
Book Dept., China Natinal Publiations
Import and Export Corporation (CNPIEC)
16 Gongti E. Road, Chaoyang District
Beijing 100020 Tel. (10) 6506-6688 Ext. 8402
 (10) 6506-3101

CHINESE TAIPEI – TAIPEI CHINOIS
Good Faith Worldwide Int'l. Co. Ltd.
9th Floor, No. 118, Sec. 2
Chung Hsiao E. Road
Taipei Tel. (02) 391.7396/391.7397
 Fax: (02) 394.9176

**CZECH REPUBLIC –
RÉPUBLIQUE TCHÈQUE**
National Information Centre
NIS – prodejna
Konviktská 5
Praha 1 – 113 57 Tel. (02) 24.23.09.07
 Fax: (02) 24.22.94.33
E-mail: nkposp@dec.niz.cz
Internet: http://www.nis.cz

DENMARK – DANEMARK
Munksgaard Book and Subscription Service
35, Nørre Søgade, P.O. Box 2148
DK-1016 København K Tel. (33) 12.85.70
 Fax: (33) 12.93.87
J. H. Schultz Information A/S,
Herstedvang 12,
DK – 2620 Albertslung Tel. 43 63 23 00
 Fax: 43 63 19 69
Internet: s-info@inet.uni-c.dk

EGYPT – ÉGYPTE
The Middle East Observer
41 Sherif Street
Cairo Tel. (2) 392.6919
 Fax: (2) 360.6804

FINLAND – FINLANDE
Akateeminen Kirjakauppa
Keskuskatu 1, P.O. Box 128
00100 Helsinki

Subscription Services/Agence d'abonnements :
P.O. Box 23
00100 Helsinki Tel. (358) 9.121.4403
 Fax: (358) 9.121.4450

***FRANCE**
OECD/OCDE
Mail Orders/Commandes par correspondance :
2, rue André-Pascal
75775 Paris Cedex 16 Tel. 33 (0)1.45.24.82.00
 Fax: 33 (0)1.49.10.42.76
 Telex: 640048 OCDE
Internet: Compte.PUBSINQ@oecd.org

Orders via Minitel, France only/
Commandes par Minitel, France exclusivement :
36 15 OCDE

OECD Bookshop/Librairie de l'OCDE :
33, rue Octave-Feuillet
75016 Paris Tel. 33 (0)1.45.24.81.81
 33 (0)1.45.24.81.67

Dawson
B.P. 40
91121 Palaiseau Cedex Tel. 01.89.10.47.00
 Fax: 01.64.54.83.26

Documentation Française
29, quai Voltaire
75007 Paris Tel. 01.40.15.70.00

Economica
49, rue Héricart
75015 Paris Tel. 01.45.78.12.92
 Fax: 01.45.75.05.67

Gibert Jeune (Droit-Économie)
6, place Saint-Michel
75006 Paris Tel. 01.43.25.91.19

Librairie du Commerce International
10, avenue d'Iéna
75016 Paris Tel. 01.40.73.34.60

Librairie Dunod
Université Paris-Dauphine
Place du Maréchal-de-Lattre-de-Tassigny
75016 Paris Tel. 01.44.05.40.13

Librairie Lavoisier
11, rue Lavoisier
75008 Paris Tel. 01.42.65.39.95

Librairie des Sciences Politiques
30, rue Saint-Guillaume
75007 Paris Tel. 01.45.48.36.02

P.U.F.
49, boulevard Saint-Michel
75005 Paris Tel. 01.43.25.83.40

Librairie de l'Université
12a, rue Nazareth
13100 Aix-en-Provence Tel. 04.42.26.18.08

Documentation Française
165, rue Garibaldi
69003 Lyon Tel. 04.78.63.32.23

Librairie Decitre
29, place Bellecour
69002 Lyon Tel. 04.72.40.54.54

Librairie Sauramps
Le Triangle
34967 Montpellier Cedex 2 Tel. 04.67.58.85.15
 Fax: 04.67.58.27.36

A la Sorbonne Actual
23, rue de l'Hôtel-des-Postes
06000 Nice Tel. 04.93.13.77.75
 Fax: 04.93.80.75.69

GERMANY – ALLEMAGNE
OECD Bonn Centre
August-Bebel-Allee 6
D-53175 Bonn Tel. (0228) 959.120
 Fax: (0228) 959.12.17

GREECE – GRÈCE
Librairie Kauffmann
Stadiou 28
10564 Athens Tel. (01) 32.55.321
 Fax: (01) 32.30.320

HONG-KONG
Swindon Book Co. Ltd.
Astoria Bldg. 3F
34 Ashley Road, Tsimshatsui
Kowloon, Hong Kong Tel. 2376.2062
 Fax: 2376.0685

HUNGARY – HONGRIE
Euro Info Service
Margitsziget, Európa Ház
1138 Budapest Tel. (1) 111.60.61
 Fax: (1) 302.50.35
E-mail: euroinfo@mail.matav.hu
Internet: http://www.euroinfo.hu//index.html

ICELAND – ISLANDE
Mál og Menning
Laugavegi 18, Pósthólf 392
121 Reykjavik Tel. (1) 552.4240
 Fax: (1) 562.3523

INDIA – INDE
Oxford Book and Stationery Co.
Scindia House
New Delhi 110001 Tel. (11) 331.5896/5308
 Fax: (11) 332.2639
E-mail: oxford.publ@axcess.net.in

17 Park Street
Calcutta 700016 Tel. 240832

INDONESIA – INDONÉSIE
Pdii-Lipi
P.O. Box 4298
Jakarta 12042 Tel. (21) 573.34.67
 Fax: (21) 573.34.67

IRELAND – IRLANDE
Government Supplies Agency
Publications Section
4/5 Harcourt Road
Dublin 2 Tel. 661.31.11
 Fax: 475.27.60

ISRAEL – ISRAËL
Praedicta
5 Shatner Street
P.O. Box 34030
Jerusalem 91430 Tel. (2) 652.84.90/1/2
 Fax: (2) 652.84.93

R.O.Y. International
P.O. Box 13056
Tel Aviv 61130 Tel. (3) 546 1423
 Fax: (3) 546 1442
E-mail: royil@netvision.net.il

Palestinian Authority/Middle East:
INDEX Information Services
P.O.B. 19502
Jerusalem Tel. (2) 627.16.34
 Fax: (2) 627.12.19

ITALY – ITALIE
Libreria Commissionaria Sansoni
Via Duca di Calabria, 1/1
50125 Firenze Tel. (055) 64.54.15
 Fax: (055) 64.12.57
E-mail: licosa@ftbcc.it

Via Bartolini 29
20155 Milano Tel. (02) 36.50.83

Editrice e Libreria Herder
Piazza Montecitorio 120
00186 Roma Tel. 679.46.28
 Fax: 678.47.51

Libreria Hoepli
Via Hoepli 5
20121 Milano Tel. (02) 86.54.46
 Fax: (02) 805.28.86

Libreria Scientifica
Dott. Lucio de Biasio 'Aeiou'
Via Coronelli, 6
20146 Milano Tel. (02) 48.95.45.52
 Fax: (02) 48.95.45.48

JAPAN – JAPON
OECD Tokyo Centre
Landic Akasaka Building
2-3-4 Akasaka, Minato-ku
Tokyo 107 Tel. (81.3) 3586.2016
 Fax: (81.3) 3584.7929

KOREA – CORÉE
Kyobo Book Centre Co. Ltd.
P.O. Box 1658, Kwang Hwa Moon
Seoul Tel. 730.78.91
 Fax: 735.00.30

MALAYSIA – MALAISIE
University of Malaya Bookshop
University of Malaya
P.O. Box 1127, Jalan Pantai Baru
59700 Kuala Lumpur
Malaysia Tel. 756.5000/756.5425
 Fax: 756.3246

MEXICO – MEXIQUE
OECD Mexico Centre
Edificio INFOTEC
Av. San Fernando no. 37
Col. Toriello Guerra
Tlalpan C.P. 14050
Mexico D.F. Tel. (525) 528.10.38
 Fax: (525) 606.13.07
E-mail: ocde@rtn.net.mx

NETHERLANDS – PAYS-BAS
SDU Uitgeverij Plantijnstraat
Externe Fondsen
Postbus 20014
2500 EA's-Gravenhage Tel. (070) 37.89.880
Voor bestellingen: Fax: (070) 34.75.778

Subscription Agency/ Agence d'abonnements :
SWETS & ZEITLINGER BV
Heereweg 347B
P.O. Box 830
2160 SZ Lisse Tel. 252.435.111
 Fax: 252.415.888

NEW ZEALAND – NOUVELLE-ZÉLANDE
GPLegislation Services
P.O. Box 12418
Thorndon, Wellington Tel. (04) 496.5655
 Fax: (04) 496.5698

NORWAY – NORVÈGE
NIC INFO A/S
Ostensjoveien 18
P.O. Box 6512 Etterstad
0606 Oslo Tel. (22) 97.45.00
 Fax: (22) 97.45.45

PAKISTAN
Mirza Book Agency
65 Shahrah Quaid-E-Azam
Lahore 54000 Tel. (42) 735.36.01
 Fax: (42) 576.37.14

PHILIPPINE – PHILIPPINES
International Booksource Center Inc.
Rm 179/920 Cityland 10 Condo Tower 2
HV dela Costa Ext cor Valero St.
Makati Metro Manila Tel. (632) 817 9676
 Fax: (632) 817 1741

POLAND – POLOGNE
Ars Polona
00-950 Warszawa
Krakowskie Prezdmiescie 7 Tel. (22) 264760
 Fax: (22) 265334

PORTUGAL
Livraria Portugal
Rua do Carmo 70-74
Apart. 2681
1200 Lisboa Tel. (01) 347.49.82/5
 Fax: (01) 347.02.64

SINGAPORE – SINGAPOUR
Ashgate Publishing
Asia Pacific Pte. Ltd
Golden Wheel Building, 04-03
41, Kallang Pudding Road
Singapore 349316 Tel. 741.5166
 Fax: 742.9356

SPAIN – ESPAGNE
Mundi-Prensa Libros S.A.
Castelló 37, Apartado 1223
Madrid 28001 Tel. (91) 431.33.99
 Fax: (91) 575.39.98
E-mail: mundiprensa@tsai.es
Internet: http://www.mundiprensa.es

Mundi-Prensa Barcelona
Consell de Cent No. 391
08009 – Barcelona Tel. (93) 488.34.92
 Fax: (93) 487.76.59

Libreria de la Generalitat
Palau Moja
Rambla dels Estudis, 118
08002 – Barcelona
 (Suscripciones) Tel. (93) 318.80.12
 (Publicaciones) Tel. (93) 302.67.23
 Fax: (93) 412.18.54

SRI LANKA
Centre for Policy Research
c/o Colombo Agencies Ltd.
No. 300-304, Galle Road
Colombo 3 Tel. (1) 574240, 573551-2
 Fax: (1) 575394, 510711

SWEDEN – SUÈDE
CE Fritzes AB
S-106 47 Stockholm Tel. (08) 690.90.90
 Fax: (08) 20.50.21

For electronic publications only/
Publications électroniques seulement
STATISTICS SWEDEN
Informationsservice
S-115 81 Stockholm Tel. 8 783 5066
 Fax: 8 783 4045

Subscription Agency/Agence d'abonnements :
Wennergren-Williams Info AB
P.O. Box 1305
171 25 Solna Tel. (08) 705.97.50
 Fax: (08) 27.00.71

Liber distribution
Internatinal organizations
Fagerstagatan 21
S-163 52 Spanga

SWITZERLAND – SUISSE
Maditec S.A. (Books and Periodicals/Livres
et périodiques)
Chemin des Palettes 4
Case postale 266
1020 Renens VD 1 Tel. (021) 635.08.65
 Fax: (021) 635.07.80

Librairie Payot S.A.
4, place Pépinet
CP 3212
1002 Lausanne Tel. (021) 320.25.11
 Fax: (021) 320.25.14

Librairie Unilivres
6, rue de Candolle
1205 Genève Tel. (022) 320.26.23
 Fax: (022) 329.73.18

Subscription Agency/Agence d'abonnements :
Dynapresse Marketing S.A.
38, avenue Vibert
1227 Carouge Tel. (022) 308.08.70
 Fax: (022) 308.07.99

See also – Voir aussi :
OECD Bonn Centre
August-Bebel-Allee 6
D-53175 Bonn (Germany) Tel. (0228) 959.120
 Fax: (0228) 959.12.17

THAILAND – THAÏLANDE
Suksit Siam Co. Ltd.
113, 115 Fuang Nakhon Rd.
Opp. Wat Rajbopith
Bangkok 10200 Tel. (662) 225.9531/2
 Fax: (662) 222.5188

TRINIDAD & TOBAGO, CARIBBEAN
TRINITÉ-ET-TOBAGO, CARAÏBES
Systematics Studies Limited
9 Watts Street
Curepe
Trinadad & Tobago, W.I. Tel. (1809) 645.3475
 Fax: (1809) 662.5654
E-mail: tobe@trinidad.net

TUNISIA – TUNISIE
Grande Librairie Spécialisée
Fendri Ali
Avenue Haffouz Imm El-Intilaka
Bloc B 1 Sfax 3000 Tel. (216-4) 296 855
 Fax: (216-4) 298.270

TURKEY – TURQUIE
Kültür Yayinlari Is-Türk Ltd.
Atatürk Bulvari No. 191/Kat 13
06684 Kavaklidere/Ankara
 Tel. (312) 428.11.40 Ext. 2458
 Fax : (312) 417.24.90

Dolmabahce Cad. No. 29
Besiktas/Istanbul Tel. (212) 260 7188

UNITED KINGDOM – ROYAUME-UNI
The Stationery Office Ltd.
Postal orders only:
P.O. Box 276, London SW8 5DT
Gen. enquiries Tel. (171) 873 0011
 Fax: (171) 873 8463

The Stationery Office Ltd.
Postal orders only:
49 High Holborn, London WC1V 6HB
Branches at: Belfast, Birmingham, Bristol,
Edinburgh, Manchester

UNITED STATES – ÉTATS-UNIS
OECD Washington Center
2001 L Street N.W., Suite 650
Washington, D.C. 20036-4922 Tel. (202) 785.6323
 Fax: (202) 785.0350
Internet: washcont@oecd.org

Subscriptions to OECD periodicals may also be placed through main subscription agencies.

Les abonnements aux publications périodiques de l'OCDE peuvent être souscrits auprès des principales agences d'abonnement.

Orders and inquiries from countries where Distributors have not yet been appointed should be sent to: OECD Publications, 2, rue André-Pascal, 75775 Paris Cedex 16, France.

Les commandes provenant de pays où l'OCDE n'a pas encore désigné de distributeur peuvent être adressées aux Éditions de l'OCDE, 2, rue André-Pascal, 75775 Paris Cedex 16, France.

12-1996

IEA PUBLICATIONS, 9, rue de la Fédération, 75739 PARIS Cedex 15
Photo PIX - Printed in France by Louis Jean
(61 98 24 1 P) ISBN 92-64-16187-2 1999